Yayori Matsui
Women's Asia

Yayori Matsui

Women's Asia

Zed Books Ltd
London and New Jersey

Onnatachi no Asia by Yayori Matsui
Copyright © 1987 by Yayori Matsui
Originally published in Japanese by
Iwanami Shoten, Publishers, Tokyo, 1987

Women's Asia was first published in English by
Zed Books Ltd, 57 Caledonian Road, London N1 9BU, UK and
171 First Avenue, Atlantic Highlands, New Jersey 07716, USA.

Copyright © Yayori Matsui, 1989.
Translation copyright © Mizuko Matsuda, 1989.

Typeset by EMS Photosetters, Rochford, Essex.
Cover designed by Andrew Corbett.
Printed and bound in the United Kingdom
at Biddles Ltd., Guildford and King's Lynn.

British Library Cataloguing in Publication Data

Matsui, Yayori
  Women's Asia
  1. Asia. Women. Social conditions.
  I. Title.
  305.4'2'095

  ISBN 0-86232-826-8
  ISBN 0-86232-827-6 pbk

Library of Congress Cataloging-in-Publication Data

Matsui, Yayori.
  Women's Asia.
  Translation of: Onnatachi no Asia.
  1. Women – Asia – Social conditions. 2. Women – Asia –
    Economic conditions. 3. Feminism – Asia. I. Title.
  HQ1726.M3813 1989   305.4'2'095   88-29781
  ISBN 0-86232-827-8
  ISBN 0-86232-827-6 (pbk.)

Contents

Preface to the English Edition

Since *Women's Asia* was published in Japan in 1987, there have been major political changes in Asia that affect and concern women. The driving force behind some changes has been peoples' aspiration and struggle for democracy. For example, in South Korea, dictator Chun Doo-hwan was toppled from power; in Taiwan, with the end of thirty-eight years of martial law grass-roots movements are springing up throughout the country; in Burma, the people's movement exploded and, even though brutally crushed, the will of the people survives; and perhaps the most dramatic event was the election victory of Benazir Bhutto and her confirmation as Prime Minister of Pakistan, the first woman political leader in the Islamic world. Even with the discouraging news from the Philippines, where President Cory Aquino confronts the New People's Army, and human rights violations continue, the tide of democratization is persistently moving forward. The voices of women in South Korea, Taiwan, Burma, and Pakistan, and throughout Asia are being heard; the rallying cry is that economic development must be accompanied by political freedom.

In spite of some progressive political changes, the vast majority of people in Asia remain desperately poor, and the women are still the poorest of them all, still the last colony, wanting and waiting to be freed from the bondage of hunger, inhuman treatment, and despair.

The reader will quickly see that the intention of this book, as it was originally designed, was to bring an awareness to Japanese people, who are enjoying abundant affluence, of the deprivation and poverty that rules the existence of millions of women, and men, and of Japan's direct involvement in their lives. It is most encouraging that some women's groups, schools, and non-governmental organizations (NGOs) in Japan are using this book as study material, and this opportunity to share the voices of Asian women with readers in the West, in other parts of Asia, and the Third World must be welcomed.

It is my hope that these voices will bring to the readers an understanding of the unjust, unequal, and exploitative systems that drain the life of these women and children, and that together we can identify and recognize our responsibility for these systems. This will call for a re-examination of our own lifestyles and a commitment to sharing in the suffering and struggle. We must unite to support actions to change these global economic structures that have such negative impacts on human life.

I must express my gratitude to Mizuho Matsuda, the Director of the Asian Women's Shelter HELP in Tokyo, members of the Asian Women's Association, and many other friends who share these concerns and who have helped produce the English edition. I especially want to thank Betty Sisk Swain, my American friend and long time resident of Japan, who prepared the English manuscript. Without her skills and understanding English-language readers might never have heard the voices of our Asian sisters. I am convinced now more than ever that sisterhood is powerful, and international!

Yayori Matsui

Introduction:
My Encounter with Asian Realities

The family environment in which I grew up was one of shared religious values, such as the equality of human beings before God, and this made my adjustment to Japanese feudalistic society very difficult. Consequently, when I was a university student, I decided to study abroad. The racial discrimination I encountered in Western society was deeply disappointing and I decided to return to Japan. A month-long journey by ship from Marseilles took me to various Asian ports on the way. This was in the late 1950s and my encounter with the reality of Asia during this journey was one of the most shocking events of my young life.

I saw unimaginable poverty. In Bombay, I saw people curled up in foetal positions dying on the streets. Noisy crowds of begging children followed me in Colombo, Sri Lanka, and squatting Vietnamese women selling food in the streets of Saigon looked exhausted. These scenes were in striking contrast to the ostentatious wealth I had observed in countries in Europe and the United States during my two-year stay there. Had I seen the poverty of Asia without having experienced the overwhelming wealth of Western Europe perhaps I would have been less profoundly affected, but I felt intuitively that somehow this wealth had been taken from Asia. In my mind's eye I could see an Asia exploited, deprived, impoverished by centuries of colonial rule and, as an Asian myself, I felt intense pain and anger.

We are all human beings, inhabiting the same planet, so why must some of us suffer so. As this question tumbled around in my head it seemed to me that the idea of human equality before God is a reality that can be applied only to white Westerners.

Returning to Japan I had to face the barrier of sex discrimination in order to get a job. Becoming a newspaper reporter was the furthest thing from my mind but, by chance, the *Asahi Shimbun* (newspaper) was the only company allowing women graduates to take employment examinations at that time. I was surprised to discover that in this job I could express my anger against injustice in Japanese society, although at that time I could not write about my own experiences in Asia.

In my writing I made it a priority to expose those who were victimized and forgotten in the process of Japan's rapid economic growth in the 1960s. I began to explore these issues from two viewpoints; of a deprived Asia, and through the eyes of women. I wrote about handicapped children as victims of the drug Thalidomide and examined social welfare issues, such as a shortage of child-care centres and the family problems of women as single parents; and of concerns about the growing population of the elderly and their needs. I reported on food safety, pesticides, defective goods, and other consumer issues.

In the late 1960s, I concentrated on environmental pollution issues. During this time I lived for a month with a fisherman's family whose young daughter was a congenital victim of Minamata disease, which is caused by mercury poisoning from industrial waste-dumping in the coastal waters of western Japan. While I was in this small fishing village, I began to question the meaning and structure of Japanese society as it began its climb to economic power.

Pollution issues also gave me a chance to turn my attention again to Asia. The early 1970s saw the spread of anti-pollution campaigns all around Japan and, accordingly, companies were forced to introduce strict pollution control measures. The government had to pass new environmental laws, and even in the courts a new concept of liability for companies charged with pollution damage was introduced. In order to avoid the cost of restricting pollution Japanese companies began to relocate polluting factories in other Asian countries: pollution then became a kind of Japanese export. For this reason the problems it generated could not be dealt with within this country's borders.

In late 1970 and early 1971 I had an opportunity to spend six months visiting the United States, Europe, and the Soviet Union in order to write about their environmental problems, such as pollution, and about organized movements concerned with these problems. This look at grass-roots movements to protect and preserve the world we live in was a deeply moving experience.

While I was in the United States I had a chance encounter with the 'Women's Lib' movement that was then spreading like wildfire. It was such a surprise! It made me question the first decade of my career as a journalist, because even though I was deeply indignant about the rampant sexism in Japanese society, I could not analyse in any systematic way its root causes. I saw myself simply as a working journalist, not a female journalist on a newspaper where ninety-nine percent of my colleagues were male.

When I returned to Japan I had confidence in myself as a woman for the first time, and decided that I would in future see my job as that of a *feminist* journalist, tackling the many problems related to sexism and discrimination against women. This was just before the United Nations Women's Decade that began in 1975 and it seemed that I could utilize this event to take women's issues away from the women's or family page, into the social issues and political pages of our newspaper. As I pursued this course it slowly dawned upon me that Japan's economic growth had been largely achieved by discrimination against women domestically, and by the exploitation and oppression of women in Asia and other regions of the Third World.

In 1974 I joined a young people's study tour called the Southeast Asia Seminar Experience on Foot, and we visited South Vietnam (which was still at war), Thailand, Malaysia, and Indonesia. This journey was my second eye-opening encounter with Asia. I was not surprised by the poverty of the people; they were just as poor as they had been more than ten years before when I had first visited those countries as a student. What did astonish me was the evidence of Japan's expansion in Asia; these countries were flooded with Japanese goods and factories. I wondered if Japan were replacing Western Europe as the colonial ruler. The realization that Japan had joined the ranks of those exploiting Asia made me very angry. The dream of a 'Greater East Asia Co-Prosperity Sphere' by military means having failed, would economic power bring success? During my three-week trip I witnessed Japan's full-scale economic expansion into other Asian countries – what Filipino Professor Renate Constantino, a strong proponent of Philippine nationalism, calls 'the second invasion'.

Throughout this trip in South-east Asia I recognized my own ignorance of, and indifference to, our Asian neighbours. That Japan's economic development had been achieved through the sacrifice of other Asians was a fact of which I had been unaware, and it shamed me. Since this turning point in my life I have been continuously involved, in one way or another, with Asian issues.

Japanese commercial journalism, which advocates so-called 'objective, neutral reporting', limited the expression of my views related to Asian issues. So, together with friends, I founded a small organization – the Asian Women's Association – which allows my personal involvement without constraint. The purpose of the Association is to examine the relationships between Japan and other Asian countries from the point of view of women, focusing on such issues as sex tourism, Japan–South Korea relations, war responsibility, Japanese multinationals, exploitation of women for cheap labour and so on. The Association also intends to challenge the discrimination and sexism inherent in the structure of Japanese society from a new feminist perspective. Women are truly the 'last colony', and thus the suffering in Asia caused by the new colonialism of First World countries can be seen most clearly through the eyes of women.

My concern for Asia extended to the Third World in general, and was placed in the context of North–South issues when I was covering the United Nations International Women's Year Conference in Mexico City in 1975. In the luxuriously appointed conference hall, one after another, beautifully dressed women representatives of various governments made speeches on women's equality. Outside the hall I saw a poor Mexican-Indian mother holding her baby wrapped in a shawl, begging in the rain. I cannot forget that poverty-stricken mother and child, they seemed to be questioning my life in an affluent society.

In the opening speech of the conference, Mexican President Echeverria said that the most oppressed women in the world are poor mothers who are unable to send their children to school or take them to a hospital for medical care. He asserted that as long as billions of poor women in the Third World are not provided with the means for survival as their basic human right, then women's liberation will never be realized.

This was also the message from Latin America, and from other Third World women in the non-governmental organization (NGO) Tribune meetings in Mexico City. They questioned United States' women's claim that men and women must have equality in an affluent society, and accused them of taking their wealth from Third World countries where poor women struggle each day just to survive. The US women were told that they should question a system that impoverishes women in the South. So acrimonious was the confrontation between Latin American and United States women that at times they physically struggled for possession of the microphone.

Listening to the debate forced me to realize that this condemnation by women in the South applies also to Japanese women, and I had to think of Japanese women as belonging to the North in this conflict of values. We Japanese women play a double role: we are discriminated against in Japanese society and, at the same time, we benefit from the exploitation of other Asian women, just as do the women of the United States. We are both victims and oppressors.

Whether Japanese women can establish solidarity with other Asian and Third World women depends on our challenging and resisting the Japanese system that oppresses them. Only a tiny minority of Japanese women take such a stand in a society where both men and women enjoy its affluence.

I frequently suffered a sense of powerlessness, especially when I began campaigning against sex tourism. There was deep hostility from Japanese men and I felt isolated at my workplace in *Asahi Shimbun*'s editorial office. Men from economically strong countries travel to buy sex from women of economically weaker countries. This North–South issue is also a facet of sex discrimination against women. To condemn sex tourism, therefore, is to challenge the exploitative structure of Japanese politics, Japan's economic system, and the sexist nature of Japanese men; this is why my attempts to pursue this matter received such a hostile response. Condemned, criticized, and mocked, I overcame this situation only by remembering the young girls who sell their bodies on the streets of Manila and Bangkok, and by calling to mind those courageous women who struggle today to eliminate inhuman sexual exploitation in many Asian countries.

At the time that I was dealing with such issues, despite hostility and harassment, I was given a welcome opportunity to work regionally, by going to Singapore from November 1981 to May 1985 (the latter half of the UN Women's Decade) as *Asahi Shimbun*'s Asia correspondent.

When our editor asked me if I wanted to be assigned as a foreign correspondent I replied, 'Yes, of course, if it is in Asia.' This had been my aspiration ever since my return journey to Japan as a student nearly twenty years previously when I had that short, never-to-be-forgotten encounter with that part of the world.

'Why Asia?' many colleagues asked. One said, 'Don't you know that stories and reports from there are not easily accepted for publication in Japanese newspapers?' But still I was determined to encounter the grass-roots of as many Asian countries as possible, to see Asia with my own eyes, to know the people, and to try to perceive relationships with Japan from their perspective. It was with such hopes that I left Japan for the Asia Bureau in Singapore.

During those three and a half years I visited eighteen countries: the three newly industrialized countries of South Korea , Taiwan, and Hong Kong; five ASEAN countries: the Philippines, Thailand, Malaysia, Indonesia, and Singapore; five countries in South Asia and the poorest: India, Pakistan, Bangladesh, Sri Lanka, and Nepal; Burma; and three socialist Indo-China countries: Vietnam, Kampuchea, and Laos; I also visited Australia. Among countries I visited most often were the Philippines, Thailand, and Malaysia.

Even in the midst of such an infinite variety of cultures a

commonalty emerged. Most of these countries shared a history of suffering under colonial rule and military aggression. Many of them are even now under an oppressive political system, such as a military government. With the exception of Australia, they are all part of the Third World and have experienced severe poverty as their economies have been dominated by those of developed countries and the superpowers. They are different countries with somewhat different systems, but their people experience the same grinding poverty.

In the beginning I was almost overwhelmed by the diversity: many different religious traditions such as Islam, Hinduism, Buddhism; plural societies encompassing different ethnic groups; differences in lifestyle, gaps between classes and castes and many different languages. All of this, as I discovered, is evidence of these countries' long history and rich cultures. Coming from a largely homogeneous culture I found this extreme diversity at first perplexing, but each day the attraction to Asia grew within me.

In many countries I could see that the burden of poverty falls most heavily on women and I recognized its many faces: in Bangladesh mothers lose nearly half their children due to malnutrition or disease; in Nepal women's lifespan is shorter than men's because of the combination of hard work and poverty; in Malaysia and Sri Lanka, women who work on plantations live in small huts that are more suitable for animals; ten- to twelve-year-old Thai girls are sold to brothels, and some were burned to death locked in the cellar of a building destroyed by fire; a woman in a Manila slum became mentally deranged because she was unable to feed her children; many Indian women become victims of rape, or of murder or self-immolation because of dowry disputes; Islamic law in Pakistan sanctions public whipping for women who transgress against its edicts.

In common with many other Third World women, millions of Asian women suffer a three-fold oppression: 1) economic, political, and military control by the developed countries of the North; 2) as working-class women, oppression and exploitation by their own dictatorial governments and ruling classes; and 3) discrimination due to patriarchal tradition. The economic development in Third World countries over the past few decades has been in the interests of the already developed countries, and has resulted only in widening the gap between rich and poor on international as well as national levels. Consequently, women are commoditized and dehumanized as cheap labour, as prostitutes, and as the poorest of the poor in rural areas as well as in the city slums.

Nevertheless, in all these countries I met determined women who began to speak out and act to rid themselves of these three oppressions. When I reflect on my experiences in Asia, my strongest memories are of the courage of those women who were challenging their fate, and that moved me to tears more than the suffering I witnessed. I shall always remember the warmth and dignity of the impoverished, elderly Himalayan village woman who had nothing for herself, yet embraced the trees and started the Chipko movement to protect the forests. She is known today as the mother of the Chipko Movement. Her compelling humanity questions the lifestyle of Japanese women who deplore the emptiness of their lives in the midst of economic prosperity.

My assignment to the Asia Bureau enabled me to cover various women's conferences in many Asian countries, and this afforded me the privilege of knowing many women who are fighting for social justice and human rights.

Immediately after my return from Singapore in 1985, I attended the Nairobi Conference to conclude the UN Women's Decade, and I noticed the difference between this conference and the Mexico City meeting of ten years before. This time Asian women were outspoken and active, which I found very encouraging. During that decade oppression and discrimination against Asian women had become more serious but, at the same time, more women were becoming aware of their situations, and during the 1980s, in most Asian countries, new women's movements were organized to work for change. Asian women are now building up networks and beginning to step forward into the twenty-first century. These are strong and determined steps toward liberation from poverty and oppression, and the goal is the creation of a new society. Listen to the real voices of Asian women, voices that are being carried on a new wind of change.

1.
From Despair to Self-Reliance:
Poor Women in Bangladesh

Introduction

At the 1983 Asian Women in the Struggle for Justice Conference in
Bombay, we were presented with a short play illustrating the plight of
poor, rural Asian women. One of the participants was Shamsun
Chowdhury from Bangladesh. About thirty-five years old, wearing a
white and burgundy sari, Shamsun took the role of wife of a poor
landless Bangladeshi peasant, played by a Hong Kong participant
wearing jeans. Labouring together with her husband at the landlord's
house, Shamsun fetches water, carries firewood, pounds rice, grinds
flour, cares for the chickens, working throughout the day with no rest.
The narrator, a Japanese, Roman Catholic nun, speaks: 'Bathed in
sweat, she spends the whole day in unceasing labour but she can earn
only five *taka*.

In the next scene Shamsun returns to her own home and finds her
child (played by a delegate from Macao) crying out, 'I'm hungry, I'm
hungry.' Since there is no food to feed the child, Shamsun goes to see a
money-lender. (The Indonesian woman who played the part of the
money-lender wore a big sign pinned to her chest to advertise her
business!) Shamsun bows up and down before the seated money-lender
begging for help but receives only an arrogant 'No.' After discussing
the situation with her husband, this small family of three pack their
meagre belongings and leave their village.

The next scene portrays their arrival in a squatters' camp in a big
city; they collect scraps of wood and begin to build a small makeshift
hut. The husband goes out to look for work and Shamsun sits with her
child in the street begging. She notices some cow dung and an idea
occurs to her. The narrator speaks again: 'She considered how she and
other women like her could get together and make cow-dung fuel to
sell.' (Several other women come on to the stage and are seen busily
pantomiming making and drying cow-dung pats.) 'One piece of cow

dung can be sold for one *taka*. Thus, poor women got together, co-operated, and survived.'

This vivid presentation of women on the edge of starvation, who moved forward to self-reliance, received much applause. And Shamsun's role as the poor woman was so impressive that these grass-roots activists, from fourteen different Asian countries, were moved to tears and laughter.

Shamsun's play was based on her own experiences as a social worker. She was born into a rather wealthy landowner family in the suburbs of Dhaka, capital city of Bangladesh, and having been brought up in accordance with strict Islamic tradition, had led a very sheltered life. Naturally warmhearted, she sympathized with the plight of beggars who came to the door of her home, and tried, whenever she could, to give food to the starving mothers and children, without her parents' knowledge. At the age of thirteen, according to custom, she was wedded to the son of another landowner, and became a mother at only fifteen years old.

Fortunately, Shamsun's husband was a progressive man who, in spite of his wealth and class, supported social reforms that attempted to solve the problems of poor, landless peasants. Shamsun became a social worker because, she said, 'I couldn't close my eyes to the injustice and inequality in our own society.' 'My parents were opposed to my activities and disowned me, but I can still continue my work because my husband understands my commitment.' She devotes herself to efforts in support of those who are deprived because of their poverty, literally working with them in the mud and dung, and helping them to rise above their indigence.

This was a real-life drama that we had seen on the stage. No matter how hard poor peasants work they cannot feed themselves, and so they migrate to the slums of the cities. Women without work have no alternative but to beg, or to sell their bodies. Shamsun's short fifteen-minute play highlighted the harsh conditions forced on Asian women due to rural poverty and urban population explosion. I was reminded of those women whom I had met in my journeys to Asian countries; especially I was reminded of the Bangladeshi women.

> Soil of Bengal,
> Water of Bengal,
> Wind of Bengal
> Fruit of Bengal . . .

In this poem the Bengali poet Tagol describes the beauty of his native land and I saw that nearly boundless delta of the Ganges River, flowing from North India through the plains of Bangladesh, to empty itself into the Sea of Bengal. It was so vast. I crossed one river after another; Bangladesh is a country of rivers. The sunset I saw from a ferry boat crossing the Pattna Ganga River was breathtakingly beautiful. Why are the people who live in a land filled with such natural beauty so poor?

The land is small, only twice the size of Hokkaido, Japan's northernmost island, but it is densely crowded with one hundred million people. After a bloody struggle, it gained its independence from Pakistan in 1971. The scars of exploitation, first by Britain, then by India, and finally by Pakistan, remain. The country was left devastated, and economic development has been very slow. It is one of the poorest countries in the world and is known as an experimental field for aid because so many governments' and non-governmental organizations are pouring huge amounts of money into it. About seventy percent of the government's budget is dependent on foreign aid.

I visited Bangladesh twice in 1982: two weeks in the spring and one week in autumn. On both occasions I made several visits to the countryside. Travelling from one village to another, I became aware of the reality of poverty, especially for the women. About eighty percent of Asian people are peasants who live in conditions of extreme poverty.

The Children's Nutrition Centre

I began my visit to Bangladesh in Dhaka, the capital city, riding in a rickshaw with a colourfully decorated canopy. The puller was a man wearing only a seamless *rongi*, a sort of wrap-around skirt, that left his sweating upper body naked. He pedalled me to the Children's Nutrition Centre located in a residental area. Mothers dressed in shabby saris, carrying babies or holding small children by the hand, were coming and going. I was astounded by the scene in a second-floor ward: near the window in the sun-room more than ten small children with swollen bellies and thin limbs were sitting very still. Their big hollow eyes stared at me from pale faces; like stone statues, they made no movements. Normally, children of this age never seem to stop moving, but here there was an uncanny stillness. These children were too weak even to move. Nearby, a young mother in a sari hugged her small, thin baby on her lap and stared vacantly.

In the main room were thirty beds for babies and small children, some so tiny they would almost fit into the palm of one's hand. The bodies of some were disfigured by a skin disease; some were blind because of a vitamin A deficiency. All these children lay quietly in their cots, watched over by their mothers whose faces were pale and expressionless. Dr Sultana Khanum, who talked with me in her clinic on the centre's ground floor, told me:

About 120 children are brought here each day from squatter areas in the city, or from neighbouring villages. About ten percent of them are suffering from malnutrition and are hospitalized with their mothers. When the centre was opened in 1975, one out of every four children died. Now, less than ten percent die: fifty-one children died last year.

She continued, 'We give two weeks of nutrition education to mothers who are not hospitalized.' She pointed to a warehouse-like building near the entrance, where inside were mothers, thin and exhausted-looking, sitting around a large pan, learning how to cook green and yellow vegetables with which to feed their malnourished children.

Even though I teach them like this, I'm not sure if they practise this at home because they do not have enough money to buy the vegetables. Unless mothers have a certain income level, medicine and health-care training will bring few results. Most of the women here have already lost children and they are very serious about bringing up the children they now have.

Dr Khanum said, 'In our country seventy-five percent of children under three years old suffer from malnutrition.' The infant mortality rate is fifty per 1,000 births (in Japan, only six per 1,000). Bangladesh has one of the highest infant mortality rates in the world, and one out of four children die before the age of five; the major cause of death is malnutrition. Even in a country free from war, many children die every day.

Red-light districts

The city of Dhaka is densely crowded, with a sea of humanity in every direction. I travelled to the city of Narayanganj, about twenty kilometres from Dhaka, and made my way through groups of rickshaws waiting for customers. Before the British colonized what is now Bangladesh, Dhaka was an old port city made prosperous by Bengali Muslims. I soon arrived at Tanbajar, one of the oldest and largest red-light districts on the Indian subcontinent. Entering the gate I saw many brothels of all sizes on both sides of a small alleyway. Barefoot children rushed up to me and the Bangladeshi photographer with whom I was travelling, signalling with their fingers and shouting, 'Pretty girl, one *taka*, cheap; pretty girl, one *taka*, cheap.' I was genuinely shocked to see quite a number of pimps who looked as young as primary-school children.

I entered a six-storey brothel near the entrance to the alleyway. Inside the courtyard, a number of heavily made-up women, wearing colourful but cheap saris, were standing around; others gazed down on us from the upper balconies. I talked with a young, slim, flat-breasted girl. Speaking in an expressionless voice, she said, 'My name is Shaheen. I am fourteen years old. I came from the village of Mymensingh about half a year ago. I don't know where my parents are.' Moving her head as she spoke her shiny earrings and bracelets tinkled. 'I take five or six customers each day, and I make twenty *taka* [about 200 yen].' Probably her parents were poor, landless peasants who were unable to feed their family, and they might have sold this daughter. They might be one of the thousands of squatter families living in the Dhaka slums.

There are about 2,000 prostitutes in this red-light district, half of them under sixteen years of age; some are only nine. These girls who are sold to the brothel when very young have no knowledge about how to get away. They must accept their situation as decreed by fate and acquiesce in the face of it.

In several of the brothels I visited, I saw a number of prostitutes with their children; a plump woman carrying her naked baby was waiting in her room for a customer. I noticed a small portable organ and a baby bottle on her bed. 'It's eight years since I came from my village; I have no more home to return to,' she said in a detached way.

Another woman, also a mother, was resting between customers. I was surprised to see a boy of six or seven years old in her room. 'May I take your photo?' I asked. She nodded her assent and, dressed in a flower-print sari, she posed with her son, her hand resting on his shoulder. As I looked at her through my camera viewfinder, my heart was grieved to see her face so depressed and lonely-looking. This woman's personal history is not unique. In her late twenties and pretty, she is the wife of a poor peasant from the village of Comilla. With her husband's consent, she decided to come here with her son because they are deeply in debt.

My photographer–guide, a resident of the city, told me: 'The people in the rural area are so poor that many of their women are coming here to work as prostitutes. They are recruited by brokers who travel from village to village. The customers come from all classes but many of them are poor men, such as day labourers, rickshaw-pullers, street vendors, who cannot afford to marry. These women also come to the city because they cannot feed themselves.'

This Tambajar red-light district is the lowest-class brothel area, which foreign tourists do not dare to visit. The women who sell their bodies here and the men who buy are both victims of rural poverty. It was truly a glimpse of hell of earth.

Rural women

Leaving Dhaka, I travelled south to the rural areas. The countryside was a vast plain of dry, brown paddies, and two-wheeled ox carts moved slowly along the roads. One village consisted only of several thatch-roofed huts located under some coconut trees. At the sound of our minibus, a number of naked, barefoot children burst out from within these simple houses. Apparently undernourished, all these children had swollen bellies and thin limbs, but they were still in better health than the children I had seen sitting so quietly at the nutrition centre in Dhaka.

Small boys of primary-school age were fishing in a nearby stream and some were cutting grass with sickles. They were working instead of going to school; only the men were working in the fields. In this Islamic society, women are rarely seen; they are confined to their homes. Even in Dhaka, receptionists, typists, tea servers, and office workers are all male. Shopping is also considered to be a man's task, except in high society, when the veiled women are escorted by a man, and among the lowest classes.

We came to a river where the ferry landing was crowded; ox carts were trying to ford the shallow water. A woman carrying a baby came up to where we were waiting our turn to board the ferry. Her face was hidden by the end of a torn sari, and she stretched out her hand to me. Other women beggars crowded around whispering, '*Baksheesh, baksheesh* [money, money]', and they were joined by women vendors shouting their wares. In order to survive, these women had to defy the strict Islamic laws and appear in public. I was told that some women who work for the local landowners could not afford the fifty *paisa* (five yen) ferry fare so that usually they had to swim across the river, fully clothed. For a full day's labour they can earn only five *taka*, which is not enough to feed several children.

In the evening, after crossing several more rivers, we finally reached the small rural town of Gournodi in the south. I had come to attend a seminar for rural women workers in South Asia, which was to be held at a Catholic centre. During this seminar I was able to visit neighbouring villages where I was always surrounded by children. The absence of women and the presence of so many children everywhere was very surprising to me.

In one village, inside one of the small peasant huts, I saw four or five women working on the floor with jute, a coarse fibre used in making a variety of things. The room was dark and meagrely furnished with only a water pot and a few plates. The women's husbands were out working in the landowner's fields.

'How many children do you have?' I asked one woman, Renuma, who appeared to be in her fifties. 'Well, six,' she replied rather hesitantly. She had borne ten children but four had died. In Bangladesh, as in many Third World countries, the difference between the number of children born and the number that survive is often quite large. When I asked her age, she was perplexed; she guessed that she was in her thirties but did not know exactly. She had never gone to school and, like more than eighty percent of Bangladeshi women, was illiterate. The literacy rate here is 14.3 percent for women and 32.9 percent for men. Renuma looked considerably older than she actually was because of frequent pregnancies, poor nourishment, and overwork. Often she had only one meal a day.

Population issues and family planning

'Why did you have as many as ten children?' was the rather rude question I then asked, and the neighbourhood housewives looked at one another. After a moment or two Renuma spoke shyly, 'I must have extra hands to help me, and when I get old, I will need someone to take care of me.'

I often saw children in this country with large cloth bags, picking up all sorts of things in the streets: garbage and pieces of wood – anything that could be used for fuel. It costs nothing for poor families to have children; there are, for example, no school fees to pay. Not only do children provide labour and can sometimes earn a *taka*, but one out of four do not survive infancy, so families never stop having children.

People in Bangladesh are poor not because they have too many children; rather they have many children because they are poor.

It is true that Bangladesh is suffering from a population explosion. The birth rate is 4.7%, which is one of the highest in Asia. Within a very short time, its population has reached 100 million. The population density in the rural areas is also one of the highest in the world. Because of this, from 1976, the government has given the highest priority to population control measures. In addition, many Western countries that offer economic aid put pressure on the Bangladesh government to implement a population control policy. The World Bank, United States Aid, and the United Nations Fund for Population Activities are three international organizations that provide as much as US$55 million annually for population control projects. 'Family planning' are words that I heard in every village, at all organization meetings, and at every conference. But only ten percent of the women of child-bearing age practise any kind of birth control.

It is said that the contraceptive pill is not suitable for women in this country because more than ninety percent of those in the rural areas are illiterate and do not understand how to use the pill. Many do not have calendars, there is no safe place to keep the pills away from children, or to keep them cool in this very hot climate. The husbands of those women who do take the pill object to it; there have been cases of divorce when the wife took the pill secretly.

Consequently, other contraceptive methods have been encouraged, promoted, or forced upon the women. One of these is the drug Depo-Provera (medroxyprogesterone acetate). This is simple to use as it is administered by injection, once every three months. The Bangladesh Association of Family Planning promoted its use and, in the 1980s it has become the third most popular method of contraception, after the pill and the condom. Depo-Provera is not, however, approved for use within the United States and other developed countries because it is suspected of being carcinogenic.

Depo-Provera was first introduced in 1974, by the People's Health Centre in the suburbs of Dhaka. But, in 1982 after it had been discovered that it resulted in harmful side effects, such as abnormal bleeding and a decrease in the flow of breast milk in lactating women, the Centre discontinued its use. The Children's Health Centre in Faridpur in the south, which had started administering Depo-Provera in 1978, also stopped prescribing it in 1982, after it was found to be harmful.

The Bangladesh government and the Family Planning Association, however, continue to promote the drug, on the grounds that the side effects are not serious, merely abnormal bleeding! Because they consider that Depo-Provera is the simplest and most practical contraceptive method, they have insisted on continuing with its use.

A critic of the use of this drug is Dhaka social worker Farida Akhatar. She is researching family planning methods from a woman's point of view and points out that excessive bleeding is a very serious problem for poor rural women.

> It is easy for women in the West to care for themselves in this situation, but poor women cannot afford to buy sanitary napkins, and they are unable to work. On top of this, there are many religious taboos that affect the lives of menstruating women. If she is a Hindu, she is not allowed to cook; if she is a Muslim, she is not permitted to attend religious activities.

Farida considers the side effects of Depo-Provera to be very serious both for economic and cultural reasons. I understood her viewpoint more clearly when I visited the village of Gournodi.

Because the birthrate is not declining quickly enough, the Bangladesh government has chosen sterilization of women as the most effective method of birth control and, in 1980, launched a 1.4 million sterilizations project as part of its second five-year economic plan (1980–85). Previously, sterilization accounted for only nineteen percent of contraceptive methods used, but the government planned to increase this figure to forty-three percent by 1985. As an incentive to undergo the operation, women were offered a sari and 180 *taka* (1,800 yen). When I was visiting a village health centre, I heard the sharp scream of a woman who was being sterilized without sufficient anaesthesia; newspapers report various instances of death due to failure of this procedure. Family planning workers were assigned monthly quotas for sterilizations, and to meet these quotas many women were virtually forced to participate. Farida told me:

> I know of a case in which a mother-in-law forced her sixteen-year-old daughter-in-law into being sterilized, in order to get the government award. Another women was operated on in unsanitary conditions, men were smoking and other relatives looking on. Treated like animals, threatened by both the drug Depo-Provera and sterilization, the poor rural women are being victimized. . . . I can never accept a method of family planning that uses Third World women as guinea pigs. Using force is neither effective nor humane. We need fundamental measures to speed economic

development, this will attack the problem of poverty itself. For now, it is more important to at least improve health care service for women. Women should be allowed to choose birth control methods themselves.

With this reasoning, Farida, in various newspaper articles, is conducting a vigorous campaign against the government's family planning policy.

There is no doubt that reasons for a high birthrate are many and varied: early marriage, high infant mortality rate, little or no education, illiteracy, unemployment, concerns of the ageing; but a high birthrate, as we have already noted, is not necessarily the cause of poverty.

Causes of poverty

We must ask, then, what are the causes of such devastating poverty? With an average yearly income per capita of only US$100, eighty percent of Bangladeshis live below the poverty line, and are unable to obtain even the minimum necessary calorie requirements. There are two important facts to realize: first, Bangladesh was exploited as a colony; and, second, just one percent of the people now own this vast land. Almost all of this one percent comprise absentee landlords, engaged in various business activities, living in big cities, and accumulating great wealth. Conversely, more than half the remaining ninety-nine percent are landless and very poor, and becoming poorer. For example, when money is needed for medical fees or a daughter's dowry, the small landholder must mortgage his land, or divide it and sell. Consequently, the small parcels of land become even smaller. Such an unequal land distribution system is the root cause of poverty in Bangladesh.

In Dhaka's exclusive residential area Gulshan, I frequently saw women dressed in beautiful silk saris, riding in expensive foreign cars. By contrast, in a slum known as Karabagan, where peasants who migrated to Dhaka from rural areas live in shabby makeshift huts covered with rags, I saw a pale-faced, exhausted-looking woman with her small children making paper bags. Outside the hut a little girl was picking garbage from a dustbin. In the cities, unemployment is increasing, and the wives of unemployed men have to work part-time. In order to survive, some have to beg on the streets or become prostitutes.

A Japanese recruiter of construction workers for the Middle East told me:

> When we advertise for a hundred workers, two or three thousand will rush to apply. To select which ones are most fit for the work, we use a physical test of carrying fifty-kilogram sand bags. Since some applicants will have not eaten for some time, they are weak and fall down. I was really taken aback when some men who were not selected came up to me and, clinging to my legs, pleaded, 'Please take me, please take me.' The unemployment situation in this country is terrible.

In this vast land, supposedly rich in natural gifts, both the cities and the villages teem with people suffering from extreme poverty.

In the South Asia Rural Women Workers' Seminar in the town of Gournodi, more than twenty grass-roots activists from seven countries met to discuss ways in which rural women might attain self reliance. Mina Malakan, a Bangladeshi woman doctor, explained that women are not only poor, but that they also suffer because they are women. She said:

> Some women come to the hospital even though they have no particular disease. They have to work very hard with not enough to eat; they lack sleep because of many children to care for; they have no family member with whom to share their problems, and they feel extremely lonely. Also, in our country, it is not so easy for women to come all the way to the hospital when they are sick. Women are not allowed to go out alone. They usually have to walk many kilometres to the hospital, nearly always accompanied by someone. Basically, women are not treated as human beings. Wives normally eat leftover food, if there is any, but no one cares what she eats. Sometimes I will ask a husband, 'If your wife gets sick and can no longer take care of the children or the family, what will you do?' The husband is embarrassed. For him, it is quite natural to think of his wife as a working machine. She is only a tool for his use, and no one can sympathize with her situation. One young girl was forced into marriage at the age of eleven or twelve. She became pregnant before her body had matured, and she suffered greatly with an extremely difficult delivery. She never recovered from the after-effects, and so she was forced into a divorce by her husband's family. Women's health is not a priority in this country.

Dr Malakar, who spoke with deep sorrow and anger as if she herself had suffered from all the ills that she had presented to the seminar, said in conclusion that it was not enough to protect the health of poor rural women, but that education and income-generating activities should be integrated with primary health care.

> This is why I started a project for women to knit shawls for sale. Before this, women hid their faces with their saris, but now they spread their saris over their shoulders and speak openly. They even carry their hand-made products to Dhaka by boat without a male escort. No one could have imagined that they could do this before.

Dr Malakar's report to the seminar participants touched receptive chords as all the participants were trying to cope with the same kinds of problems. Some were so moved they stepped forward and silently embraced her.

Steps towards self-reliance

Steps to liberation by village women who are poverty-stricken and oppressed by discrimination are slow, but I did see some women in various villages beginning to move under their own power. Amidst the despair in this poor country, I also saw signs of hope.

On another occasion I travelled north from Dhaka by jeep to Jamalpur. We crossed shallow rivers without bridges; we put planks down where there should have been roads and we pushed ox carts with wheels stuck deep in the mud to open a passageway. It was such a struggle to move on that we did not reach Jamalpur until it was dark. The following morning I visited several villages, guided by Masaaki Ohashi, a worker from the Japanese volunteer group Shapla Neer, which in Bengali means 'white lotus'. This is a non-governmental organization for overseas co-operation; Masaaki Ohashi supports poor peasants in organizing unions, and he is also determined to encourage and assist the women in their self-help projects.

We visited one of the peasant huts where I saw middle-aged women seated on the floor working with jute fibre. Their movements were barely discernible in the dim light of the sun shining through the cracks in the wooden walls of the hut. These women were core members of the village Women's Committee. Mr Ohashi explained:

> About twenty members of the committee each donate 1 *taka* or a

handful of rice every week. In this way they have already saved up 2,000 *taka*. A member can then borrow as much as 100 *taka* as seed money for her project, and the ten percent interest that she pays on the loan becomes the resource of the co-operative.

If these women were to borrow from the village money-lender, he would charge them thirty percent interest. Through the co-operative women have raised their own funds and developed income-generating jute handicrafts.

In another village different projects were underway, for example, weaving rope from coconut shell fibre, hiring out the rice-polishing machines during the farmers' off season, or raising goats. Shapla Neer co-operates in organizing the poorest women in the villages to begin their own self-help projects. Women who, previously, were not treated as human beings now exhibit a great deal of pride in their achievements of self-reliance by supporting each other in co-operative work. They now speak out and no longer hide their faces.

These projects are attempts to humanize aid to people at the grass-roots level, no matter how minimal this might be in terms of the money involved. In comparison, the Official Development Aid (ODA) projects funded by First World countries are pouring huge amounts of money into the poorest countries, and the poor people are poorer for it. They are neglected, humiliated, and impoverished as human beings.

On my return to Dhaka, I went to see the shop, called *Aron*, where all kinds of jute fibre handicrafts are sold: bags, handwoven tablecloths, embroidered cushion covers called *nokushikata*, Christmas cards made from straw, and so on. All these items were colourful and beautiful, and I recalled the scenes of the village women, seated on the floors of the dark huts with their babies on their laps, working quietly. And as I touched these handicrafts, I sensed the warmth of the women's hands that not only provide life for themselves but also support the economy of Bangladesh. The country is dependent on these hands.

Now and always I will remember these handmade items into which these peasant women wove, stitched and painted their despair and hope, and I will always remember with deep affection the women who live on the soil of Bengal.

2.
Women Plantation Workers:
Colonial Rule, Past and Present

As the aeroplane descended, the Malay Peninsula came into view and I was entranced by the beautiful green carpets of trees planted so precisely and looking very much like a chequerboard. This is Malaysia, a country of plantations, where the lush green under a tropical sun is so pleasing to the eye – and, where the people who live here are so poor.

Today, a thirty-six-year-old mother, Kamachi Aseu, and her children, are gathering up the fallen red fruit of the oil palm tree. She wears a dirty T-shirt, and a sarong that fails to hide her thin legs. She looks exhausted; her eyes express resignation and depression. Because of the rain, the dark fields look even darker and Kamachi and her children have taken shelter at a small Hindu shrine. Everything about her embodies the despair of the women plantation workers.

Oil palm and rubber plantations: Malaysia

In November 1984, Professor Ramasamy of Kebangsaan University and two other Indian Malaysians took me to visit a rubber and oil palm plantation in Rawan, only a half-hour drive north from Kuala Lumpur, capital city of Malaysia. Entering the gate I saw shabby wooden linehouses, each one connected to the next in long rows, clustered around a Hindu temple. There were about thirty women and children, all dark-skinned Tamil people, waiting for a truck that would take them to the oil palm harvest fields. We travelled to the fields by car, driving up and down the hilly roads for about six kilometres, passing rubber trees on the right-hand side and oil palms on the left.

Kamachi was there, working with her children who ranged in age from five or six to about ten years old. They were picking up the fallen red fruits and putting them into the tin cans they carried. In the morning the male workers cut the 70–80-centimetres-wide clusters of fruit from the tree tops and it is the work of the women and children to gather the fallen fruit.

The rain was coming down harder and harder. Kamachi, sitting in the small shrine, reluctantly and in a soft, indistinct voice told me:

> At six o'clock in the morning I go to the rubber plantation to tap trees, and I stay there until around noon. Then, in the afternoon, I go to pick up oil palm fruit until it gets dark. Even working as hard as we can, my children and I can fill only six or seven bags.

She is paid only 70 Malaysian cents (70 yen) for each bag so her daily income from the oil palm fields is only 4 or 5 Malaysian dollars (400–500 yen).

Kamachi's parents had migrated from India and settled in Sentul, a slum area of Kuala Lumpur, where she was born. Her parents died when she was young; she was unable to go to school and, at the age of thirteen, was married to a plantation worker in Rawan. Mother of five children, she is now a rubber-tapper.

Rubber-tree tapping is women's work. She has to rise at five in the morning to go to the rubber-tree forests where she cuts the bark of the trees with a small knife, collects the liquid that drips into cups hanging around the tree trunks, and delivers this to a nearby factory. The children have to help her as she must tap 500 trees each morning. The price of rubber has recently fallen and rubber trees are being replaced by the oil palms, a more profitable yield. This is why the women have to work at harvesting the oil palms in the afternoons.

Kamachi's husband also works on this same plantation, and the family's entire income amounts to only about M$300 monthly (30,000 yen). It is not easy for a family of seven to live on such a small income. Kamachi has never been back to Kuala Lumpur and the neighbourhood where she was born and raised, even though it is only thirty kilometres from where she now lives. She cannot afford the bus fare of M$2.8, and knows nothing of the dramatic changes in the city of her birth.

Poverty's vicious circle

I visited Kamachi's home inside one of the barrack-like linehouses where ten families live. Her neighbour Rechumi, a thirty-two-year-old housewife, had come home early and already had started to cook the evening meal. Rechumi is the mother of Segaran, the twelve-year-old boy who had been collecting oil palm fruit with Kamachi and her children.

In a very dark kitchen that had no electricity, silhouetted in the light of the fire where the rice was cooking, I could see a small boy curled up on the floor. This was Segaran's brother, a mentally handicapped child. Their father is in prison because he injured someone when he was drunk. Rechumi has been struggling to survive, to support her seven children, one of whom is disabled.

'Segaran is very helpful and is doing well in taking on his father's responsibilities,' Rechumi says as she goes out to fetch water from the nearby pond and returns, covered with sweat. She looks almost ten years older than she really is.

In the living room, a small space with a concrete floor, Rechumi's mother-in-law sits staring blankly out of the window. Sixty-five years old, her face is wrinkled and worn from many years of hard labour. She said:

> I have worked enough already, and I feel I have done my duty, but I have no peace of mind because I am worried about my grandchildren's future. I cannot afford to send them to school, and I have no hope that they will be able to escape from this miserable life.

She had more than ten children and now has nearly sixty grandchildren and six great-grandchildren. But only the three children of her eldest son, who is a little better off than her other children, are attending school. With regret, resignation, and anxiety, this old woman is nearing the end of her life without any hope that her family will be able to break out from the circle of poverty that has bound four generations.

In Malaysia, a quarter of a million people from 150,000 families work on rubber, oil palm and coconut plantations. Since each family averages seven or eight members, more than one million people live on the plantations, more than half of whom are Tamils of Indian descent. The export crops they produce earn about forty percent of the country's foreign currency.

These plantation workers are supporting industries basic to the nation's economy, but their living and working conditions are miserable, as I saw from my brief visit to Rawan. Low wages keep them below the poverty line throughout their lifetimes. They suffer from long working hours, that start at four or five o'clock in the morning; they have poor housing with neither electricity nor running water, and with only concrete floors. Children must work instead of going to school. Their health suffers due to the overuse of pesticides, and from a high rate of alcoholism. Truly, people in the closed-off world of plantations live in dire poverty.

The culture of poverty

The culture of poverty – that is to say, indifference, self-abasement, irresponsibility as parents, drinking, the lack of mutual help, subjugation of women, and so on – are all interwined to make the poor Indian's life even more miserable. I feel ashamed as an Indian. This culture of poverty is not, however, the responsibility of the Indians, but is created by various factors beyond their control.

So spoke an Indian Malaysian, Mr Jayakumar, in his analysis of the cultural aspects of poverty among Malaysian Indian plantation workers at the 1983 International Conference on Modernization and Ethnic Cultural Identity in Kuala Lumpur, organized by the Malaysian Social Scientists Association.

First, the legacy of British colonial policy in the history of plantations still has its influence. In the early twentieth century, Britain brought in as many as 80,000 poor peasants each year from South India where they were living in starvation conditions, also under colonial rule. Transplanted to the Malay Peninsula, these peasants were cruelly exploited as plantation workers. They were so poorly paid that they had to search the garbage for enough food for survival, and were subjected to brutal physical punishment, such as whipping. These workers, deprived of their last shred of human dignity, were treated like slaves.

As a result, a 'culture of passivity' was created among the workers and remained even after Malaysia gained its independence. Physical punishment has been abolished, but plantation workers can still be intimidated by transfer to less productive areas, by retrenchment, and by arrest.

On our way back from the plantation in Rawan I asked Professor Ramasamy, 'Why do the workers remain silent when they are left out of economic development and such miserable conditions are imposed on them?' He said: 'The only solution is for the workers themselves to unite and stand up for their rights. At least they should speak up in their local chapters even if they cannot dissolve the 'yellow' [pro-government] plantation workers unions. They are all dissatisfied and want to act, but they are too oppressed. It is not an easy thing for workers to organize themselves.

Turning towards his two friends in the car with us, Professor Ramasamy said, 'This gentlemen has just been released from prison after serving an eleven-year sentence, and this friend was in prison for three years. Both of them were arrested because of their activities in organizing a labour union among plantation workers.' In this way workers are still threatened and prevented from organizing.

During the international conference mentioned above, Professor Jayakumar referred to a second factor in the creation of a culture of poverty: the Indian caste system, which predates the plantation system and was brought to Malaysia from India by the workers themselves. Most of these forced labourers were poor, landless peasants of the lowest caste or outcasts from South India who, according to Hindu teaching, were considered to be unclean or untouchable. Consequently, it seemed natural to treat them as sub-human. This cultural background was fully exploited by the plantation owners to deprive the workers of any spirit of resistance, a quality that should be present in all human beings.

Kamachi, Rechumi, and Rechumi's mother-in-law – and all the women whom I met at the Rawan plantation – expressed this inbred apathy, which has resulted from a history of colonial rule, a feudalistic and traditional culture of discrimination, economic exploitation, and violation of human rights.

On the plantations, where the culture of poverty is rooted, the women are those most victimized. In Hindu culture, women are considered inferior to men, and forced to be dependent on them. The men, who drink *toddy* (coconut wine) to forget their problems, often behave violently towards their wives. Since they themselves live such oppressed lives, they compensate for this by oppressing their women, the ones in the weaker position.

For some time after World War Two, partly because communist influence was strong, militant labour unions were formed that succeeded in slightly improving wages and living conditions for plantation workers. But because these unions were also dominated by men, women's issues were hardly addressed. The ratio of women to men among plantation workers steadily increased and, in the 1980s, approximately fifty-seven percent of the workers are women. In spite of this, their suffering as women has never been alleviated; on the contrary, their situation seems to deteriorate.

Women plantation workers are physically exhausted by frequent pregnancies and childbirths. Families average seven children because they need as many workers as possible; nurseries where small children are left are poorly equipped with not even any toys; husbands often waste meagre incomes on drinking, and alcoholism is very common. The work of women is very hard, carrying water and collecting firewood; they are constantly in ever-increasing debt. Miscarriages are common, because even pregnant women must climb ladders to tap the rubber trees high off the ground. They also suffer all kinds of health problems, especially those due to exposure to dangerous pesticides, including paraquat, which causes eye disease, bleeding and nausea. They are in frequent danger of rape because they must work alone in the rubber-tree and oil palm forests. They are constantly fearful of losing their jobs because many of them are stateless and carry only red identity cards indicating this. These are major problems women plantation workers face – all of them serious, and all difficult to solve.

Testimony of a plantation manager's wife

My understanding of the women plantation workers' problems was confirmed in a discussion with a woman who lives on a plantation in Teluk Intan, about a two-hour drive north from Kuala Lumpur. Her husband, a Malay university graduate whose speciality is agricultural economics, is employed as a plantation manager by the Danish company owner. She is an Indian and a middle school teacher, very active in the consumers' movement. She has participated in investigations into child labour on the plantations and has recently become interested in the circumstances of women living on the plantations. The difference between her living conditions – a pleasant colonial house with a swimming pool – and those of the women plantation workers has become painful for her.

> When my husband and I came here to live, I played tennis, read books, and enjoyed a leisurely life. But I felt something different when, at a party, I overheard some men gossiping in amused tones about the rape of a worker's wife. Soon after that, happening to look out of the window I noticed a woman coming up the lane, breathing heavily and carrying a load of firewood. At that time, something changed inside me. I became aware of my indifference to the conditions of the women workers on this plantation, and how they suffer in contrast to my easy pleasant life. Since then, I have tried to be in touch with them and their situation here.

Now actively involved in the life around her she works to improve the children's nurseries, and campaigns to prevent poisoning from pesticides.

> This plantation is better than others because even an old people's home is provided. But, the circumstances of life for the workers is

still very harsh. I put pressure on my husband to improve the conditions here and he always has a headache nowadays because he is caught between the owner on one side and me on the other.

Considering her husband's position I cannot use her name here, but I was deeply moved by her courage in making every effort to support women workers' rights. The Indian men who had earlier escorted me to the plantation at Rawan had shown me how difficult it is to organize plantation workers because those who do so risk imprisonment. And I recognized, too, that this manager's wife is also risking her livelihood in her effort to improve workers' lives.

Malaysia's relations with Japan

Malaysia, claiming remarkable economic development but where, nevertheless, its plantation workers are forgotten and isolated in pockets of poverty, has very close relations with Japan. Professor Ramasamy related an historical connection that was quite unknown to me.

> During World War Two, the Japanese occupation forces in Malaysia caused extreme pain beyond description to Indian workers. Among them, the most cruelly treated were the workers mobilized for the construction of the Thai–Burma railway, known as the 'Death Railway' because of the great numbers of workers who died during its construction. On the plantations, many still talk about their husbands, fathers, uncles, friends, who never came back from Burma.

Largely unaware of this, the Japanese are today concentrating on closer and closer economic relations.

The products of the plantations in Malaysia are necessary for Japanese daily life, but most Japanese do not realize this. Japan imports most of her rubber from Thailand, but fifteen percent of higher quality rubber comes from Malaysia as does ninety-seven percent of Japan's imported palm oil. The volume of palm oil imports has increased each year, and the demand in Japan's markets has increased ten times over that in the 1970s. Palm oil is used in making margarine, edible oils for instant noodles and for all kinds of snack foods. The products that are served on the heavily laden tables in Japan have been produced by the hard labour of Kamachi and her children. Relationships between producers and consumers are invisible because they are widely separated, but their dependence on each other is increasing.

Tea plantations: Sri Lanka

This invisible connection between the rich consumer and the poor producer is also evident on tea plantations in Sri Lanka. The ancient Sri Lankan capital of Kandy, home of a famous Buddhist temple, is surrounded by vast areas of tea plantations, like a rippling green sea. The over-arching blue sky presents a stunning sight.

The green landscape of tea bushes was dotted with spots of colour from the saris of women tea pluckers. They went silently about their work as I approached, heads covered with cloths, and huge baskets on their backs. Their dark faces were dripping with sweat that fell on to their drenched and faded saris. Taking little notice of me, they concentrated on their work, trying to pluck more than the twelve-kilogram daily quota, as even one gram more would add to their earnings. Tea plucking is women's work because of their small and nimble fingers. Tea accounts for half of the export earnings of Sri Lanka so the production of 'Ceylon' tea is dependent on these women's fingers.

Cebrai Yanma, just home from a long day's labour in the tea fields, having already taken her basket of tea leaves to the office to be weighed, told me, 'I got 15 rupees today, but those who picked just the twelve-kilogram quota got only 10'. Cebrai had been working on the Garaha tea plantation since she was ten years of age. A short woman, her many years of hard labour under a hot sun have left her face full of wrinkles and her eyes are full of sadness, and although she told me her age was forty-nine she looks nearer sixty years old.

Cebrai lives in a shabby shack where the roof and windows are covered with plastic sheets to keep out the rain. She and her family occupy one small room without any lighting. She cooks on the floor, and when the evening meal is finished and cleared away, the family sleeps there. Cebrai was married at the age of eighteen, but her husband died many years ago; she has had to raise their five children alone. Two of them have moved to the capital city, Colombo, to work, and Cebrai continues the struggle to survive with her three remaining children.

'What in your life gives you pleasure?' I asked her. She smiled and, after a moment, answered, 'Well, when my sons come home from time to time.'

Cebrai gets up each morning before sunrise, to fetch water, carry firewood, and prepare breakfast; she works all day on the plantation and comes home in the evening to repeat the morning chores and care for her children. Since this is the only life she has known for forty years, it is little wonder that she has difficulty in calling to mind any particular pleasure. She has been deprived even of the expectation of any pleasure in her daily life, surely something to which all human beings are entitled.

'Slaves of slaves'

'Plantation women are the poorest of the poor and the slaves of slaves. They are the most oppressed people in our country, and are deprived of all their rights,' says Kumari Jayawardena (*Exploitation of Women in Plantations – Tamil Women Workers on Tea Plantations*, Women's Education Centre, Colombo). In Sri Lanka, as many as 350,000 women work on plantations, representing forty-two percent of the nation's women workers, the largest labour group in the country. The tea and rubber produced on these plantations are the country's most important exports and provide the major contribution to the national economy. Despite this, of all workers women plantation workers are the most abused and suffer extreme hardships.

As Cebrai told me, their wages are extremely low – fifteen rupees a day at best – even lower than those paid to men workers. Especially hard hit are single parent families like hers; sometimes she can work only two or three days a week during a drought and she and her children then face starvation. The women are unable to provide education for their children, thus the illiteracy rate on the plantations is seventy-five percent, twice the national average in a country where the overall literacy rate is among the highest in all Asia. Infant and maternal mortality rates are also higher on the plantations, because many of the women are anaemic due to chronic malnutrition.

As Kumari Jayawardena reveals, socially, plantation workers are subjected to discrimination because they belong to the lower castes in the Tamil community. They have little freedom to change jobs; labour union organizing is very difficult; and many Tamils do not have Sri Lankan citizenship.

Tamil women's history

The severe exploitation of plantation women has a long history, beginning in the 1880s when Tamil women were brought from South

India to tea and rubber plantations in Sri Lanka as forced labourers by British colonists. It was colonial policy to utilize women as workers because, as Kumari Jayawardena puts it, 'they are cheap and docile, and can produce the next generation of workers'.

The women were forced to walk long distances from the interior to the coast of South India, where they were crammed into slave ships and brought to the northern coast of Sri Lanka (then Ceylon). From there they were again forced to walk long distances over rough territory to the tea plantations located in the central highlands. Many of them died of exhaustion, or from diseases such as malaria, before they reached their destination; and many of those who did reach the plantations died within the first few months. This illustrates the horror of forced migration. Economically, those women who survived the 'death march' and went to work were ruthlessly exploited, as well as oppressed by patriarchy. In Jayawardena's words: 'these women were doubly exploited, as wage-earning workers and as housewives responsible for children and carrying out domestic duties without compensation, all for the support of the plantation economy, which continues to this day'.

As we have noted, most of the tea plucked by women under such severe working conditions (that are themselves violations of their human rights) is exported. Even though half of the plantations are now publicly operated, the processing and marketing is still controlled by Lipton, Brooke Bond, and other major British tea companies. The Ceylon tea, mixed with African and other teas, is sold at maximum prices in markets all over the world, realizing huge profits. Consumers are attracted by the beautiful packaging, but the fragrance of pure Ceylon tea is missing from these blended products. Each cup of tea contains elements of multinational corporation profit, the pleasure of the consumer, and the lamentations of the women tea pluckers.

Today, Cebrai is plucking tea leaves in Sri Lanka and Kamachi is gathering oil palm fruit in Malaysia. Both women are part of a global exploitative structure. They live in different countries but they have much in common. Both are Tamil, descendants of poor workers taken out of South India to serve British colonial interests. The poverty of South India (also a result of British colonial rule) was brought to Sri Lanka and Malaysia along with the workers, and still exists today. Thus, these two women share the same history, and both are part of the present plantation economy that accommodates the interests of the developed countries at the expense of the women's human rights. The products that result from their sweat are exported and consumed in

First World countries and their labour is closely related to our day-to-day life in Japan.

This plantation agricultural system, profitable for developed countries, is on the increase. Former colonial administrations have been replaced by multinational agribusiness conglomerates. Not only tea, palm oil, and rubber, but coffee, cocoa, pineapples, sugar cane, bananas, and corn are also being produced on plantations. The prices of these primary products are influenced by world markets, and are decreasing. In the early 1980s, world sugar prices suddenly fell, partially due to the production and popularity of chemically produced sweetening agents in the West, with the result that in Negros Island, in the Philippines, 450,000 sugar plantation workers lost their jobs; including family members, nearly three million people still face starvation. Around 150,000 children are suffering from malnutrition, and many young girls are being sold into prostitution in Manila and to other countries.

Banana plantations: Philippines

In the late 1960s, four large agribusiness corporations (three from the United States and one from Japan) transformed vast farmlands into huge banana plantations on the island of Mindanao in the Philippines, and began to export bananas, mainly to Japan. Before World War Two, Japan had consumed bananas from its then colony Taiwan, and after the war, had imported them from Central and South America. Today, ninety percent of the bananas consumed in Japan are produced in the Philippines. Until this change occurred, bananas were an expensive luxury for the wealthy and sometimes for the sick, but nowadays they are one of the most inexpensive fruits available. But the Mindanao plantation workers who cultivate this fruit suffer from very poor nutrition, and they themselves eat only rice and fish soup.

In 1985, I visited one of the banana plantations in the suburbs of Davao in southern Mindanao. There were about 1,200 workers there, 200 of whom were women; the men cut and carry the sixty-kilogram bunches of bananas, and the women work at the packing plant.

The fruits are carried by conveyor belt to rows of water tanks to be washed, one by one, by a group of women who obviously get very wet, and, because they must stand to do this task, quickly tire. The fruit is next sprayed with chemical pesticides to prevent infestation during shipment, and finally, another group of women paste the tiny 'Del Monte' labels on the bananas. The payment for this tedious and tiring labour is only 900 pesos (10,800 yen) each month.

'When I worked on the farm I was free to grow as much food as I needed for myself, but now I get only a cash wage. My life is very hard because prices on goods have gone up,' said a middle-aged woman as she continued to wash bananas. Here is a structure where the farmers become poorer and poorer as the farmland they once used to cultivate their own food is now used to cultivate food for consumers in the developed countries.

Not far from the packing plant I saw a large clearing – this was a small airport for crop-dusting planes. I was horrified to learn that pesticides now banned in Japan and other developed countries continue to be used here. The people are worried about the effects of pesticides on health, because half-naked children playing under the hot tropical sun often contract skin diseases, and pregnant women frequently suffer miscarriage.

As I walked around in the hot air of the banana plantation, I thought of this unjust economic structure in North–South relations. While the people in the Third World are deprived of their farmlands and turned into low-wage workers, and when even their health is threatened, they produce food for the enjoyment of people in the industrialized countries.

Similarly, hunger in Africa is also related to the development of plantations. Great plains of prime farmlands are used to cultivate crops for export while local people go hungry. African people cannot eat corn because it is exported as animal feed, eventually to become succulent beefsteak and be consumed by members of affluent societies. It was frequently pointed out in forums at the 1985 United Nations Women's Decade International Conference at Nairobi, that the development of the plantation economy has resulted in increased hunger for all, but particularly for women, who usually eat the leftovers. We must give greater consideration to the plight of these women workers who suffer such hardships on plantations throughout the Third World. Clearly, the problem arises out of the South's forced dependency on the North.

3.
Women Workers in Modern Factories:
Impact of Japanese-style Management

Introduction

It was midnight in the factory and uniformed women were silently assembling tiny electronic parts; the only sound was the low hum of machinery. Most of these women were Malay, with some Chinese, some Indian.

Suddenly, there was a sharp scream, 'A ghost is in the toilet!' A woman worker began to tremble and fell to the floor crying and screaming. Women working near her were astonished, and tried to hold her but her limbs were flailing wildly and kicking anyone who came near her. Eventually a number of women together calmed her down and carried her away. The factory at midnight was less silent for a time.

'It was a horrible scene. Somehow they got the woman out of the factory and avoided an outbreak of mass hysteria,' Fatima Daud told me describing this scene that she had witnessed. Fatima Daud, a Lecturer in Social Anthropology, University of Malay, took a job for six months in 1977 at a Japanese electronics factory in the Sugai Way export processing zone in the suburbs of Kuala Lumpur as part of her doctoral research (Social Economic Problems of Women Workers in the Japanese Electronic Factory).

The twenty-year-old Malay woman who had been overcome by hysteria had been working in that factory for more than a year. Feeling stress and fatigue, she and her friend visited a doctor who advised her to take a two- or three-week holiday. She asked her manager for some time off but was allowed only two days. In her lodgings later that evening she began to scream, 'I don't want to live here any longer. I don't want to work in the factory. I want to go home.' The following night the same thing occurred, leaving her exhausted. On the third day, pale-faced, she returned to the factory, and while in the toilet, had another attack of hysteria.

In early Malay society, before the advent of Islam, people were at times afflicted with *amoq*, a kind of psychological disturbance. From usually very gentle people long-suppressed feelings would suddenly burst out; men would resort to violence, killing or injuring people, and women would become hysterical. In the 1970s, during the process of industrialization in Malaysia and Singapore, there were frequent reports of mass hysteria among Malay women workers in Western and Japanese multinational modern factories. Fatima Daud's 1977 research indicates that incidents of mass hysteria were reported in all twenty factories she studied.

In a well-known incident in Singapore in the mid-1970s, a United States multinational (General Electric) had to close down for three days because of mass hysteria among migrant women workers from Malaysia. The corporation was forced to call in a *bomo*, a traditional healer, to exorcise the 'bad spirits'.

There were also several cases of mass hysteria in a Japanese toy factory in Singapore in the 1970s and early 1980s. According to the Japanese manager of this factory:

> Only Malay women have this hysteria, even though women from different ethnic groups are working on the same assembly lines. It happens suddenly; one woman falls into hysterics, then other women who look into her eyes fall down, one after another. It's a sort of panic that is completely out of control. Although recently it has occurred less often.

Those women who come from the *kampong* (Malay village) exchange free lives as young girls in rural areas, surrounded by natural, fresh greenery, for concrete factories in big cities where their lives are dominated by the buildings and machinery. As adolescents, and mentally volatile, those who cannot adapt to the radical change in environment

> especially those women who have personal problems such as trouble with family or boyfriends, tend to succumb to hysteria. When we call in the *bomo* to pray, or we make the toilet area brighter, mass hysteria no longer takes place. And of course, since industrialization has developed, women workers are getting used to the new environment.

The toy factory manager said this with relief.

Fatima Daud, however, produced quite a different analysis:

Women workers feel like robots. Day after day, their work is monotonous, repetitious, and boring. Continuous surveillance by the boss, the fatigue of long hours and night work, strict regulations that range from going to a clinic to how to take holidays, extremely poor housing conditions, interference in their private lives, and loneliness with no one to counsel. The accumulation of these daily dissatisfactions and resentments finally explodes in the form of hysteria. It reflects the alienation of workers under the assembly-line system. They are, after all, targets of exploitation. The gathering of workers to organize labour unions to change this system is prohibited. There is no channel by which workers can express their grievances.

A Japanese factory in Kuala Lumpur

Sugai Way, the export processing zone near Suban International Airport in Kuala Lumpur where the factory I visited in 1983 (which belonged to one of the top Japanese corporations in the world) was located, was opened in 1972. There were fifteen multinational plants in this zone, nine of them Japanese-owned. In the one I visited condensers and tuners were assembled, and ninety percent of the products were exported. There was a staff of eleven Japanese, including the general manager, and of the 1,150 employees eighty percent were young women.

The first thing I discovered was that their wages – M$200 (20,000 yen) per month – were extremely low. Their labour is intensive and as the factory operates on three shifts, they are frequently called upon to do late-night work.

The hostel for women workers located in a run-down area, like a slum, is a ten-minute walk from the factory. I climbed a narrow staircase and knocked on the door. In that cheap, four-roomed apartment house lived sixteen workers.

Jamila, a nineteen-year-old, who appeared to be the leader, told me, 'I'm from a *kampong* in Pahang. I got this job three years ago by introduction from my friend who is also working.' She looked relaxed in a T-shirt and sarong. Two other women came out of the kitchen where they had been cooking the evening meal; they spoke frankly about their situation.

From their monthly salary of M$200, they each pay M$20 (2,000 yen) for rent, but as they can walk to the factory they have no transport costs. They have a simple breakfast, sometimes only a cup of tea, and eat lunch (dinner, if they are working the night shift) in the factory canteen where they can get a set meal for M$1. Usually they take turns cooking supper, Malay or Chinese food, for themselves.

'Even though my salary is very low, I have to send money to my family. That's why I have to save. It's not so easy,' said Jamila, who comes from a farming family and is the eldest daughter of eight children.

There was almost no furniture in their room. The only colour was a bunch of artificial flowers on a cheap vinyl cloth covering their dining table. There were fewer beds than occupants. At night those on day shifts sleep in the beds of the night-shift workers, and some sleep on mattresses on the floor. Some women workers commute from shabby huts in the squatter areas. In that sense, the hostel is a better place in which to live. The women not only want to forget their loneliness in the city, having left their home villages behind, but living together is much more economical.

'What do you think about your present life?' I asked the women. Jamila seemed to be speaking for all of the women when she said, 'We don't expect much so we're okay-la' (Malaysian speakers often append 'la' to words) and shrugging her shoulders, continued, 'We cannot acquire any skills, so this is not the type of job that we want to do forever. I wish I could find a nice man to marry.' At this the women exchanged knowing looks.

They are all eager to find boyfriends and so they put away the sarong that is worn in the village, wear a Western-style dress, and buy cosmetics to make up their faces; they spend their meagre incomes and make every effort to look like attractive modern women. They do not want to marry a man their parents have chosen for them in the *kampong*. It is understandable why they take this husband-hunting so seriously. While I was visiting the hostel, two of the women residents who had finished their night work were out on dates.

They behave this way because they need distractions from their work as well, according to Fatima Daud's research. Many women told her that they disliked their jobs. They mentioned various reasons which in order of the highest number of responses included: 'It's boring; night shift is hard; no chance to use brain; cannot do important things; prejudice against factory-women workers: cannot learn skills; too busy; low wage; tired.' As many as ninety-two percent of the women are ashamed of being factory workers because, as Fatima Daud explained:

They are often called 'mina current' [electric woman]. This means hot or sexy woman, or immoral woman. This is the image. Women workers in electronic products factories are looked down on by society. Another reason is that they think their jobs are inferior even to those of farmers who can at least make their own decisions. In other words, they feel helpless working under a boss with power to order their lives. They feel themselves to be merely parts of some machine.

They have strong aspirations for marriage because they are anxious to get out of the factory as soon as possible. In fact, the turnover of women workers is very high, and the average employment time span is short. But this is convenient for the companies as well; these women workers are expendable.

Industrialization under Malaysia's new economic policy

Rich in natural resources such as rubber, tin, timber, and oil, Malaysia is a multiracial society comprising Malays, Chinese, and Indians. In 1970, a new economic policy, *Bumiputra* ('son of soil' policy) with the goal of eradicating poverty and reducing the economic gaps between races, was adopted. An export-oriented industrialization policy was promoted, and foreign corporations were invited to build factories. Export processing zones were established in Penang, Kuala Lumpur, Melaka, Johor, and other places, one after another, and industrial estates (zones) were also designated in many places. Electronics and textile industries developed rapidly. Seventy to eighty percent of the workers in these two industries are young, unmarried women and about 100,000 women, most of them from rural areas, work in the electronics industry alone.

'Men go to work; women stay at home.' Such division of labour by gender is a common traditional value shared by all the races: Malay Muslims, Confucian Chinese, and Hindu Indian. Usually, the women will work until they marry and continue only as long as they can manage both job and family. Consequently, women as workers are seen as cheap labour, not full-time but half-time with no dependant family allowances, and only as supplementary-income producers. But they also have nimble fingers and can do monotonous work. It is very convenient for companies to employ docile women who are more easily controlled than male workers, because electronics industry workers are prohibited from organizing unions.

The migration of huge numbers of women from villages to modern factories related to world markets is now taking place in Asia, and indeed in the entire Third World. But does this lead women in the direction of independence and liberation? Certainly these young women who once led subservient and dependent lives as members of an extended family, ruled by patriarchy in the rural villages, now have some money of their own. And no matter how small the wage is, it brings with it a certain amount of freedom and independence; in this respect it may be a step in the right direction. Women workers are, however, finding a patriarchal system of personnel management in the factories: the section chiefs and other managers are all men, and the women must work under men's instructions and orders. As Noeleen Hazer, Women's Programme Director of the Asia Pacific Development Center in Kuala Lumpur, pointed out in her 1986 book, *Working Women In Southeast Asia, Development, Subordination, and Emancipation*, traditional values such as subordination to authority, diligence, honesty, discipline and self-sacrifice are encouraged in order to raise productivity levels. Thus, the factory is thought of as a family and women workers as members of this family. They are taught by their boss, who assumes the role of father; he supervises their behaviour, and prevents their misbehaving.

Japanese multinationals

The Japanese multinational corporations make very clever use of traditional concepts of women and values to raise productivity and increase profits. Since the 1970s, Japan's direct investment in Malaysia increased dramatically; sometimes more than twenty companies would begin operations here within a single year. In the 1980s, Prime Minister Mahatir launched a 'Look East – Learn from Japan' policy. He said, 'Western Europe is in regression while Japan is making progress. Let's learn from Japanese management and work ethics.' Thus Japan is considered to be a model for economic development, and is the biggest foreign investor in Malaysia with more than 400 companies; eighty percent of the workforce is women.

The image of the Japanese corporation among the Malaysian people, however, is not very good. Working conditions and salaries are considered to be better than local companies, but worse than Western multinational companies. One Sunday morning I visited the women workers' hostel at Senawan Industrial Estate in the suburbs of Senemban, an hour's drive south from Kuala Lumpur. The women were having a day off and kindly invited me to their rooms. Each room was furnished with a double-decker bed, and the only decorations were colourful batik dresses, neatly folded on the shelves.

> I worked at a Japanese lighter factory before, but I left after only three months, and I've been working in an American electronics factory for three years now. Why did I change jobs? Because I made M$5 a day at that Japanese factory, but now I earn M$8. Besides this, the Japanese were always ordering us to work, work, work. I felt as if I were being constantly watched. When sometimes I would talk, my Japanese boss would scold me. 'In Japan, everybody works very hard,' he said. When he was away, sometimes all of us would just stop working.

This is what twenty-one-year-old Farida, wearing a blue T-shirt and sarong, told me. She came to work in the city because she got tired of the hard work on a rubber plantation in her village. She appears to be a very responsible young woman; perhaps because she is the eldest of a family with five children.

Another young woman, twenty-one-year-old Delima, nodded in agreement:

> I've been working in a Japanese electronics factory for three years, and every day I'm staring into a microscope. In the beginning, I suffered from terrible headaches. Many women quit their jobs here because of damaged eyesight, but I couldn't find any other better job.

Delima's starting salary was M$6, and even now, three years later, she earns only M$7.50 per day.

> Prices of goods are rising, so life is hard. I work the night shift to make an additional M$4, even if it is exhausting. Altogether, I can earn a little more than M$200 a month, but I have to send some money to my family. I am really hoping for a raise. The Japanese don't like labour unions and I can't make any demands. I'm afraid of getting laid off.

Long hair reaching to her shoulders, Delima is a very charming Malay woman. Her two younger sisters work in the same American electronics factory as Farida, where meals and transport are subsidized. In this sense, the treatment is better than in the Japanese factory.

Another reason for Delima not changing her job is that she already has a boyfriend and is planning a wedding ceremony in her native village. When these young women talk about boyfriends, they suddenly become lively. 'I want to meet a nice man and get married. That is my dream,' said Farida. They all nod in agreement. 'Do you know any nice young Japanese man, because he is bound to be rich!' Everyone bursts into laughter. Perhaps this was her honest wish.

In *Malaysian Women*, published in 1983, editor Evelyn Hong of the Consumers' Association of Penang has made a comparative study of Western and Japanese multinationals, and local companies.

> In European and American electronics factories, management encourages their female workers to emulate stereotypical versions of the affluent and modern Western woman. Female workers are encouraged to participate in sports activities; they are also encouraged to have boyfriends and dates. This socialization process culminates in an annual beauty contest and grand ball usually held in an exclusive hotel in the city. For workers from traditional rural villages, this socio-cultural environment is completely different from their own restrictive cultural background.

On the other hand, Evelyn Hong says that:

> Japanese companies encourage their female workers to be gentle and passive women. Visits to Japanese factories clearly indicate that their socio-cultural system is closely based on the traditional Japanese factory system. Here the manager is portrayed as an authoritarian father figure, but one who cares for the welfare of his employees. He is concerned about the cultural development of his female workers, and that they should internalize tenets of obedient behavior and passive subordination. Workers are required to memorize company mottos and songs. They are trained to be good disciplined workers through regular exercise drills and sports activities. Women workers are encouraged to emulate stereotyped images of the refined and passive Japanese woman by tutoring them in beauty grooming and cooking skills.

As for local companies, she says:

> In the present situation where young Malaysian women prefer to work for foreign multinational corporations instead of locally-owned small companies, due to the better salaries and attractive

working environments in multinationals' factories, these local companies are faced with difficulties in getting and retaining their female workers.

This comparison of three categories of factories seems a little too simplistic, but the fact is that this image of Japanese multinational corporations is already well-established, not only in Malaysia, but also in other Asian countries. Instead of encouraging a goal of independence and emancipation for women workers, Japanese companies provide them with a place of control and oppression.

Japanese-style management and women

The situation of women workers in Malaysia is very similar to that of women workers in Japan itself. They are given the meanest jobs and are never given an opportunity to develop a career. Because they are cheap labour, they are expendable, and there is a high turnover as they themselves choose to quit.

This assessment was given by Wendy Smith in fluent Japanese when I visited her. An anthropologist from Monash University in Australia, she is married to a Malay scholar and lives in Seremban.

As a student in Japan in the late 1970s, her thesis research was on the professional and family life of women doctors in residential and downtown areas of Tokyo – 'Family and Job'. She was surprised by the low status of women in Japan. Her interest then turned to industrial relations and management of Japanese companies, and she did research on Japanese multinational corporations in Malaysia. Given the opportunity freely to visit a Japanese food factory for one year as an employee, she was able to investigate thoroughly both Japanese managers and engineers; and at the same time, closely observe Malaysian female workers.

Building on these personal experiences, she has published several articles on the status of women in Japanese factories. Because the Japanese management system is glorified by Western economists as the secret of Japan's economic growth, and because her research subject was the impact of Japanese management on Malaysian women workers, it has attracted much attention in Malaysia where the government is taking a 'Look East' policy. Few would question the accuracy of her observations as her personal qualifications include fluency in Japanese and Malay languages, and personal experience of employment in a Japanese factory.

Wendy Smith pointed out that:

> So-called 'Japanese management' has three basic supporting pillars: lifelong employment, seniority system, and a company house union, all of which are supported by family ideology. This is applied, however, only to male regular employees of big corporations; only thirty percent of employed workers in Japan. Sub-contract workers, temporary workers, part-time workers, especially women, are left out of this system.

This illustrates the reality of the Japanese management system based on a dual labour market.

She went on to say:

> The low status of women workers is an indispensable factor of the Japanese management system. The majority of female workers in Japan are young women who work till marriage or childbirth, and middle-aged part-time workers who come back to a job after the children grow up. Their average wage is about half that of male workers; they are merely expendables at the bottom of the employment ladder. In order to maintain a solid lifelong employment system, the major characteristic of Japanese companies, it is necessary to have such women workers who can easily be hired and fired, as a cushion.

Even with the new Equal Employment Opportunity Law, in effect since 1986, only a handful of women who are blessed with a strong will, ability, good health, and convenient family situation, are promoted and treated equally with male regular employees.

The majority of Japanese women workers are still targets of exploitation as cheap labour at the bottom, the same as before. In spite of the new law, the dual structure of the labour market, as Wendy Smith pointed out, has not changed basically. In addition, the law is creating a split among women.

Now in her early thirties and mother of two children, Wendy Smith confirms what I have noticed for a long time:

> In Malaysia, where thousands of women are employed by Japanese companies, it is vital to have a deep understanding of these companies. Japan is exporting everything, including discrimination against women. This is the problem.

In her paper, presented at a seminar – 'Management, Technology, and Industrialization, A Lesson From Japan' – in Kuala Lumpur in 1984, she challenged the myth of uniqueness in the Japanese management system, pointing out that:

the so-called 'Japanese management system' is exercised only in large companies. Capitalist corporations of any country that try to make a profit by controlling workers practice a similar system. The quality control circles that workers form to compete for better quality, or the zero defects movements, are called Japanese-style, but these ideas originated in the United States.

She also considers that:

To put too much emphasis on the uniqueness of Japan is a sort of strategy on the part of companies that want to impose Japan's feudalistic traditions of obedience on their workers. If one explains co-operative management–labour relations or sex discrimination in Japan from the standpoint of Japanese culture or Japan's ancient traditions, the listener is fooled into accepting these concepts as inevitable factors in Japanese company structures.

Criticism against Japanese company policy that expects women workers to be gentle and passive, and that provides an oppressive environment within which to work, is frequently heard at women's conferences in Asian countries. For example, at the 1983 'Asian Women in Struggle for Justice' conference in Bombay, the 'Industrial Women Workers' session discussed how to deal with the personnel management of women workers in Japanese factories. One of the participants was a Roman Catholic nun, Christine Tse, active in tackling human rights issues as a staff member of People's Progress Center in Hong Kong. She thought it to be absolutely vital to know about the Japanese management system that turns workers into robots without their realizing it, and consequently, in 1982, she published a pamphlet *Reflections on Japanese Management, Letters to a Woman Worker*. Sister Christine says:

When I investigated electronics factories in Hong Kong and in South Korea, I criticized the 'invisible control' that prevents female workers from exercising a critical view of their companies. After that, I went to Japan and learned about the more clever control methods of the Japanese companies. There, workers are forced to take on the identity of their companies. Even though they might be dissatisfied with company policy, it is not easy to express such feelings in the atmosphere that is created.

She is worried about the recent influx of 'Japanese-style management' into American and other multinational corporations in many Asian countries.

Multinational companies of the world relocate their plants in the developing countries in order to make maximum profit and cleverly control their workers with a Japanese-style 'magic hand'. It is vital that women workers in Asia resist this; speak up and stand up in solidarity.

Sister Christine is concentrating on establishing networks of Asian women workers as she travels around in various countries as a member of the Committee of Asian Women Workers(CAW).

Philippine export processing zone

In contrast to Malaysia, where the political atmosphere appeared fairly calm, and where women in the factories at times released their pent-up feelings of oppression in mass hysteria, in the Philippines, the people's movement was in full swing. Women workers were protesting against oppressive conditions, even participating in unlawful strikes. I visited the Bataan Export Processing Zone where the Marcos regime had invited so many foreign multinational corporations with the incentive of a 'no tax, no strike' policy, and heard about the general strike there.

This zone is in the town of Maliveres, located about 170 kilometres from Manila on the southern tip of the Bataan Peninsula, well known because of the historical 'Bataan Death March' of World War Two. There was a view of Corregidor Island, scene of a hard-fought battle of that war. I was escorted by two women from the Christian Workers Center, and they seemed quite tense as we passed Filipino soldiers who gave us hard looks as we went through the gate of the processing zone. We walked around inside the spacious compound where some fifty modern factories were operating.

The factories of thirteen different countries were located there, with the Japanese owning the most. It so happened that the eleventh Japanese factory I visited was having its opening ceremony on that day. The shining new plant, which would produce disposable cigarette lighters, had already installed machines, and 150 young female workers, all wearing jeans, were on hand to give a warm welcome to the visiting Japanese President and his wife. A Roman Catholic priest sprinkled holy water, and the conveyor belt started moving. It was the beginning of the production of six million lighters a month to be exported to the USA, Europe, and Australia. The President looked very happy at the smooth start of his second overseas plant (the first was located in Taiwan). He was cheerful and friendly as he spoke to the women workers; he was really trying to be kind.

> The Japanese management style that considers the company as family fits the national character of the Filipino people, to whom the family is very important. Since employees are treated like sons and daughters, they naturally feel loyal to the company. This is why Japanese companies are doing very well here in the Philippines.

The public relations officer at the export processing zone administration flattered Japan.

I was visiting this office to get some general information on the zone and picked up a brochure, 'Philippine Export Processing Zone'. It carried a message from the administration office chief that glorified Japanese companies:

> Japanese companies that are operating in this zone are setting very good examples, providing good working conditions, appropriate management, technological know-how, and development of the company. We are ready to co-operate with you so that you can start operating without delay. We try to make profit for you quickly. Please come to our zone.

'But you had a strike, didn't you?' I asked the public relations man. He answered, 'It's true, we've had about ten strikes in the past ten years, but we try to deal with labour through dialogue, and we speedily resolved last year's strike. We are making efforts to improve workers' housing conditions which are the cause of their grievances,' he explained rather apologetically.

A strike in the processing zone

Actually, even Japanese companies with a reputation for co-operative management–labour relations are not exempt from a strike. It is a well-known fact that 'it is difficult to form a labour union in a Japanese company', but, in the Ricoh Watch factory, where nearly 2,000 people are employed, workers tried to organize themselves into a union and it was banned; the workers then went on a protest strike. 'They were agitated by the labour boss, "Oralia Family",' the Japanese manager said bitterly when I called on him at the factory. He continued to heap abuse on Mr Felixbelt Oralia, then the Chairman of KMU (May First Movement) the most militant labour union during the Marcos regime. He was a pioneer in the Philippine labour movement, and died in 1983, aged seventy-nine. His son Roland succeeded his father as chairman, and was assassinated in December 1986.

The first general strike in this processing zone occurred in June 1982, and was initiated by a strike at a Japanese plastic bag factory, Inter Asia, a joint venture of Mitsubishi Trading Co. and a Filipino partner. The management wanted to increase the number of looms for which each worker was responsible from four to five, then to six. The workers became very angry and went out on strike. A worker recalling the circumstances said:

> We have only a twenty-minute break for lunchtime. There is no time even for a smoke after eating. We are forced to work many hours of overtime in extreme noise and dirt. Our working conditions are already inhumane and management proposed to further intensify our labour, and this we could not accept.

The workers began to picket even though they knew it was forbidden in the zone. This was in May 1982, and on the twelfth day of picketing, the Labour Ministry ordered them back to work, but they refused. On 1 June, the police and strike-breakers were sent in. The pickets were harassed and almost washed away by fire hoses; the fifty-four workers who resisted were arrested.

'When we saw the workers being arrested, we were furious. Labour leaders from several factories talked together and decided to support Inter Asia workers' struggle. In this way, the support strike was begun.' Women workers returning from the night shift to the women workers' centre outside the zone fence related their personal experiences of the strike, one after another.

'We never thought that we would have such power.' Lena, a twenty-year-old worker in an American garment factory, spoke with such pride about how they started the strike in her factory that day.

I clapped my hands as we had decided beforehand, and others responded with their own clapping. Everybody stood up to see what was happening, and I shouted, 'Let's go outside.' Then, three pregnant women rushed to the door and all the rest followed. The security guards couldn't stop a thousand women from leaving so we succeeded in our walkout. We ran to the zone administration building and joined workers from other factories in a sit-in, demanding the release of all the Inter Asia workers.

And this is how the 5 June 1982 general strike started.

The reason these workers were not afraid of going to gaol if they went on strike was because of their dissatisfaction with their working conditions, low wages – about 700 pesos (8,400 yen) per month – and the hard labour, and also because their living conditions were so miserable; these grievances were accumulating.

The numbers of workers who surrounded the administration building increased until about 15,000 had gathered. More than half of the 24,000 workers in the entire zone participated in what was the biggest general strike since the zone had been opened, and it continued for three days; most factories were completely shut down. This unprecedented strike to protest against violations of human rights by multinational companies, in an export processing zone where strikes were banned under martial law, was a severe blow to the Marcos government.

Two months later, seventy-nine-year-old KMU Chairman Oralia and more than fifty other labour movement leaders were arrested, and the law prohibiting strikes was strengthened. The 'Bataan experience' however, had been shared among workers, and the courageous action of the young women workers has become a legend.

Commuting from the slums

In the late afternoon, I left the processing zone and crossed a small wooden bridge with a large crowd of women workers, all wearing T-shirts with various company names printed on them. 'Please come and see our hostel,' said Lena, and she took me to a workers' quarters near the beach in the town of Maliveres.

The hostel was a simple wooden barracks built on the mud; a very shabby-looking toilet was located some distance from the living quarters. There was no bathroom so the women had to bathe in a nearby stream. I entered one of the nine houses, climbing wooden steps, and sat on the floor of a two to three square metre room. I could see the ground through the cracks in the floor, and each time I walked, the whole house shook. 'This is my house, my room,' said Lena, seated on the floor. Four women workers live in this small room. There is no desk, no chair, in fact no furniture at all. On the veneer wall hangs a picture of the Virgin Mary and a poster advertising Japanese cosmetics; all dimly lit by a kerosene lamp. 'This is really a slum,' I thought.

From such primitive surroundings women workers commute to modern factories on the other side of the fence. This is the only life that these young women workers know. This is how they spend their youth.

Living in big houses with six or eight rooms, with a driver and servants, the Japanese factory managers' feet have never touched the ground in the slum areas where their women employees live. I asked the same questions about workers' housing conditions of every Japanese businessman whose company I visited in the export processing zone. And the answer given was always in substance the same, delivered with noticeable indifference:

I have heard that the condition of their housing is deplorable, and that even if the sanitary conditions are improved, some of the children would still get malaria. But all these problems are really the responsibility of the Philippine government, aren't they? As a matter of fact, in this country, the living conditions of the workers in the export processing zone is not particularly worse than others; many of the people live in slum-like areas.

A manager of a Japanese textile factory emphasized;

In this country full of jobless people, companies in the export processing zone employ as many as 24,000 people and generate 600 million yen per month in products. Therefore, they make a big contribution to the economy of the country and to the community.

He did not, however, mention how much profit these companies take out of the country.

One by one, Lena's room-mates returned to the hostel; they sat on the floor and Lena began to sing. All of them joined in singing English songs, Tagalog songs, many different songs; some were passionate love songs. The Filipino people love to sing and it seems that they will do so at any time, any place. 'Since we are human beings, we just want to live with joy; we just want to be happy,' said Lena, smiling. Their last song was 'An Bayanco', (My Country) the song of national liberation; it had a sweet, sad melody.

Since the end of the 1960s, over sixty export processing zones have been established in more than fifty developing countries. Over one million people are employed in them, of whom seventy percent are Asian and the majority are women. They share the one hope: 'I want to live as a human being.' With this hope they sit day after day in front of conveyor belts, microscopes, sewing machines. The products they make are sent to us in the developed countries. And this creates the link between our daily lives and the women factory workers in Malaysia and in the Philippines.

4.
Migrant Woman Workers:
Abuse and Isolation

Nursemaids in Singapore

In a house on Mayer Road, in one of the wealthiest residential areas on the east coast of Singapore, a thirty-two-year-old Filipina named Cathy works as a maid. She is a short, brown-skinned woman wearing a T-shirt and jeans. In the quiet late afternoon we sit on the veranda of the apartment where she is slowly rocking a sleeping baby in a hammock. The baby wakes and is fretful; Cathy takes her up in her arms and kisses her cheek. 'Shizu is so darling that I forget homesick,' she says with a warm smile. Her English is very good even though she speaks with a strong Filipino accent. Soothing Shizu as if she were her own child, Cathy begins to tell me about herself. A typical Filipino woman, she is friendly and frank.

Four-months-old Shizu is the daughter of a Japanese businessman who employs Cathy, and his American wife who is working on behalf of refugees. 'When I am looking at Shizu, she reminds me of my own four children that I left behind in my home country,' said Cathy.

Why did the mother of four children have to leave them and come to Singapore to work? Cathy was born in Visayas, in the central part of the Philippines, one of the most economically depressed areas. Her father is a primary school teacher, and her mother works for the local government. Cathy went to college and studied to become a laboratory technician but, even with her training, it was difficult to get a job because the Philippines is full of unemployed people. Finally, she was hired to work in a nature conservation bureau, but her salary was only 400 pesos (4,800 yen) per month.

She married a local government official, but her husband was also poorly paid and even though they were both working, it was difficult to raise four children. This is why Cathy began to consider going abroad as a migrant worker. Her sisters-in-law were already working in Singapore as maids. 'I heard that women who had migrated to Saudi

Arabia had dreadful experiences, so I chose Singapore as I was told it was a safe place to work.'

Cathy's father was strongly opposed to her plan to work abroad. '"What a pity that a college graduate has to become a maid; she is not in good enough health to do this kind of work," my father said, and he tried to pressurize my husband into not letting me go,' Cathy said.

She was so determined, however, that she took a day-and-a-half boat trip to Manila to apply at an overseas employment agency for a job. The introductory fee was 9,000 pesos (18,000 yen). Two months later she received a telegram saying that she would be permitted to leave the country, and telling here where her employment would be. In 1983, she was finally on her way to Singapore.

Her employer was Chinese and Cathy was unable to communicate with the family. Badly mistreated, she became depressed. 'I couldn't even eat. I had no heart to write letters to my family.' She disclosed no further details and was silent. She might have experienced a severe emotional shock. Unable to remain with this family, she finally ran away. She had been employed on a two-year contract, and if she could not fulfil the terms of that contract she had no other choice but to return home.

Fortunately, before she left she was introduced to her present employer and, after spending some time at home returned to Singapore in January 1984 to begin working for this new family. 'The wife of my present employer is very warm and kind; I'm very lucky,' Cathy smiled. She earns Singapore $300 and $50 allowance each month (together a little less than 40,000 yen), which is average for domestic helpers here. Sunday is her day off.

'On Sunday I go to mass in the morning, and then to the Botanical Garden. This is the meeting place for the Filipinas and I can see my sister-in-law, cousins, and friends.' On Sundays the Botanical Garden in Singapore is crowded with Filipino women; they have lunch together, and sing and play guitars. It is really a holiday scene where the maids from the Philippines can rest and enjoy themselves. For Cathy, it is also a time for meeting with her relatives; her aunt, who was a teacher for many years, and six other family members are working in Singapore. They get together to forget the loneliness of living in a foreign country.

Cathy usually leaves early on Sunday to have time to write letters to her family.

Even on a working day, after I finish my job, I write letters to my children about school, study, play, behaviour, and such ordinary things. It is quite natural for a mother to be concerned about these issues. Fortunately, my mother-in-law is taking good care of them. My elder sons go to school and make very good marks. I am encouraged.

This mother of three sons, aged ten, eight, and seven, and a three-year-old daughter, is concerned about her children all the time. She carries their photographs with her everywhere she goes. 'When I left home, my children saw me off and all of them were crying. It was very, very hard when my daughter Sherila cried, "Mummy, don't go," and clung tightly to me. When some friend is going home I always send toys to my children.' Usually cheerful Cathy hung her head in tears.

Without education you cannot get out of poverty. I'm working hard now not only to earn my living, but also to save for the children's education so that they can grow up to be good citizens. My husband has recently written that he also wants to migrate for work to the Middle East. I have made up my mind to continue working here for another two years after this contract is up. Both of us are ready to sacrifice ourselves for the future of our children.

A college graduate mother has to bring up someone else's child far away from her own, and her husband is also planning to leave the family to work elsewhere. Such a case where family members are living and working in different places is not at all exceptional in the Philippines.

Since the Philippine government decided to have a manpower export policy in the first economic development plan beginning in 1978, the number of migrant workers has increased. Now, it is said, more than one million Filipinos are working abroad; it is truly a country dependent on overseas migration. Men go to countries in the Middle East as construction workers, and women go to many countries all over the world as maids. Like Cathy, more than 7,000–8,000 Filipinas are working as domestic helpers in Singapore. And in Hong Kong, which is even closer to the Philippines, more than 30,000 women in 1988 were working as *amah* (Cantonese for maid).

Maidservants in Hong Kong

I met migrant women in Hong Kong too. On a Sunday morning I took the Star Ferry from Kowloon to Hong Kong Island. The ferry was crowded with Filipinas, all chattering away in Tagalog or accented English. I talked with two women who were sitting next to me. Aida, twenty-six years old, in a red blouse and jeans, a tropical beauty with attractive black eyes, who had been working in Hong Kong for three years, said:

> I come from Bataan. We are a large family with eleven children, and my father has been working in the Middle East for several years already. I'm working as a maid for a British family and earn HK$1,700 (50,000 yen) a month. I send as much of this as possible to my family. My mother at home is not in good health and I am worried about her. I try to encourage her by writing letters very often.

Aida, in common with many Filipinas, is part of a widely scattered family, but she looked very cheerful and was considerate of her younger friend, twenty-three-years-old Gurlie.

Gurlie had been in Hong Kong for only two or three weeks. She wore a white blouse and skirt, and was shivering in the rather chilly spring air. Her three elder sisters had preceded her here so four members of her immediate family are now migrant workers. 'I'm going to meet my elder sister today and will borrow a sweater, so I'll be all right,' said this pretty young woman with a bright smile.

> I graduated from college this spring, and had wanted to become a teacher, but the salary was so low, only 1,000 pesos (12,000 yen) a month, that I couldn't get married. My fiancé, a university graduate too, is also unemployed. And that's why I decided to come here and work as a maid because I can make about five times as much money here.

Aida and Gurlie got off the ferry and headed straight towards St Joseph's Cathedral. I went along with them and, on the way, we passed by Statue Square, which was crowded with Filipinas. There were food stalls, vendors of all kinds of daily necessities, and street photographers. It was like a picnic ground on a holiday. Friends and relatives were gathered in groups, some showing letters, some reading magazines from home, some eating, and all of them looking relaxed. It was a similar Sunday scene to that I had witnessed in Singapore's Botanical Garden.

We made our way through the crowded square, climbed the steep slope, and reached the cathedral to attend the mass. We pushed our way up the stairs and entered a chapel where the several hundred seats were immediately filled. The choir members were Filipinas and, with the sound of the organ, a British priest began the service. Aida and Gurlie knelt and bowed their heads in prayer.

Both in Hong Kong and Singapore maids from the Roman Catholic Philippines fill the cathedral every Sunday. They pray for the health and safety of their scattered families, and for strength for themselves to endure in a foreign country in spite of their difficulties. Their faith supports them. In fact, it becomes a necessity. Both those who are mothers and whose children have been left in their home countries, and the young unmarried women, are placed in strangers' homes in a foreign country. They all experience solitude, anxiety, and emotional pain. In addition, they have to deal with so many practical problems; they _must_ depend on God.

The 'Filipina Migrant Workers Mission' is located at St Joseph's where the women are able to receive counselling. In the Mission's published report various problems are mentioned: very high fees to agents for introductions to jobs, and forced remittance of fifty to seventy percent of their income. (Citizens who are migrant workers are required by government to send a certain proportion of their earnings back to the Philippines through government banks. Exchange rates are computed to favour the banks, and fees for this transaction are charged to the workers.) Problems abound: low wages, non-payment of salary, cheating, long hours, too few holidays, poor meals and housing, violence, sexual harassment, interference in privacy such as prohibiting telephone calls and visits from friends. Since most of these women have had to borrow money, in one way or another, in order to pay large fees to the employment agents in advance; if they return home without finishing the contract period, they are unable to repay this money. Employers can take advantage of women in such weak positions, and violations of their human rights occur frequently.

Catholic Center shelter

In Singapore, in the spring of 1984, a forty-year-old French priest, Father Arotcalena, heard of the distress and concerns of the Filipino maids who came to mass, and opened a shelter in a two-storey bungalow near Geylang, a red-light district. In the big, bare living room I met this large-framed priest, dressed informally in slacks and a short-sleeved shirt, chatting with some tiny Filipinas. The telephone rang continuously and, each time, he stood up slowly and responded to the caller with warmth and kindness. He told me that about five women every week come to the Catholic Center for shelter or counselling; many of the cases are complicated and difficult to handle.

On the day I visited the shelter there were four women there. 'They are all big smiles now, but when they came here they were depressed and frightened,' Father Arotcalena said. His open, cheerful personality, unlike the conventional picture of the typical priest, must have been very comforting to those women.

'Look at the bruises all over my body,' said thirty-one-year-old Louisa whose faded T-shirt showed her neck and arms. Four years previously her husband had been killed in a car accident and she was left to support her own three children, the oldest being thirteen years old, as well as a child of her late sister. She decided that there was no other way to earn enough to feed her family and so had come to Singapore in June 1984, leaving the children in her mother's care. 'I heard about a friend who had been to Saudi Arabia and was raped. So I decided to come here, to Singapore, because I thought it would be quite safe. But I have had terrible experiences and such bad luck.'

Louisa's Chinese employer is the owner of a coffee shop and has five children. The second son, thirteen years old, is mentally disturbed, and on one occasion when Louisa was frying food, he suddenly poured the boiling oil over her. On another occasion, when she was taking a nap, he threatened to attack her with a knife. Louisa was most afraid of the eighty-year-old grandmother who always scolded her if she were in a good mood, and when in a bad mood, would beat her or throw things at her.

> She threw anything – sausages, eggs, even plates – at me. I was so scared. Finally, one midnight I ran away and called the Center, and now I am here. I was not even treated as a human being. After two months I couldn't stand it any longer.

Louisa was resting and recovering from her injuries while she looked for another job.

Another Filipina, thirty-three-year-old Soldes, thin and with long hair, was also a widow, and had six children. She had borrowed 11,000 pesos (132,000 yen), mortgaging her small farm to pay the agent to secure a job for her. But she was dismissed after only three weeks in Singapore, allegedly because of her poor English. She was neither paid for the three weeks' work nor provided with an air ticket home, which is why she had come to the Center for help.

'Next time,' she said, 'when I come back for employment, I will use a reliable agent. In the Philippines, it is extremely difficult for women like me, with children, to find a job. And even if I am hired, the wages are too low to feed a big family.' Soldes is a strong-minded mother, struggling for survival despite her misfortunes.

Since its opening, only six months previously, several hundred housemaids had been accommodated in this Centre. More than half of their problems were concerned with non-payment or cheating in wages; the next most frequent grievance was violence, then sexual harassment. Some of the women had been raped, and one of them had been forced to massage her naked employer for ten minutes every morning.

A woman lawyer in Singapore, thirty-one-year-old Ngap Bung Chin, who herself employed a Filipino maid, noticed a woman who was working for a Chinese family in the same apartment building. This Filipina always seemed to be hungry, and would slip into Bung Chin's apartment and ask for food. She was forced to serve mahjongg players until after midnight each evening and then had to get up at four o'clock in the morning to wash clothes. She was underfed and, after several months, hardly recognizable. 'There are still Chinese who stick to the old-fashioned idea that employees are to be exploited to the extreme, and economic development notwithstanding, human rights consciousness lags far behind in Singapore. These two factors are the causes of Filipino maid abuse here,' Bung Chin said.

In Singapore, even though generally women are active participants in society, and even though the number of working mothers is increasing, there are not enough child-care centres. Consequently, more than 20,000 foreign women, not only from the Philippines but also from Thailand, Malaysia, Indonesia, and Sri Lanka, are caring for these children; and the numbers steadily increase. Usually, however, the mass media reports only employers' complaints. 'It is only recently that the media has begun to report on the various human rights issues relating to these foreign maids.' The Singaporean speaker lowered his voice. 'They are supporting the economic development of this country by doing the really menial jobs such as cleaning the toilets, washing dirty clothes, and changing the diapers of the babies and old people.'

In Singapore, foreign domestic workers are not allowed to organize themselves; all citizens' movements, rallies and demonstrations are strictly prohibited. In this sense, Hong Kong is less restrictive, and a domestic workers' union has been formed and has succeeded in improving working conditions and wages. For example, salaries for foreign *amahs* have risen each year: in 1985, they rose from HK$1,650 and HK$1,800 to HK$1,800 and HK$1,950. There have been campaigns to prosecute abusive employers, and a *Filipino Helpers' Handbook* has been published, which includes practical advice urging workers to 'know about our rights and solve our problems'.

Migrant workers' wives

Philippines

It is not only migrant women who suffer; migrant workers' wives who stay at home also have their problems. In 1981, an organization, KAIBIGAN (Friends of Overseas Workers) was formed in the Philippines. Mr Mon, a staff member of this organization, took me to visit the Paco district in Manila. We walked through a labyrinth of small lanes, which had been covered with wooden planks because of the flooding from waste water, and reached a huge slum area crowded with small, shabby huts. The men of most families living here were working in the Middle East.

We had to stoop to enter the home of Leo Justiza, a thirty-six-year-old migrant worker who had recently returned from a three-year job in Jordan. The space inside the small, rough, wooden house was cluttered with TV sets, stereos, and suchlike, in various stages of repair. Leo Justiza told me:

> I was working in a United States multinational cement factory as an electrician; about 1,500 workers are employed there. Working in such intense heat was very hard, and I got tired of eating chicken three times a day every day. If we complained, we were threatened with being sent back home. The salary was not bad, however, and I made US$525 (126,000 yen) a month, so I stuck it out and did my best. Here I cannot earn even 1,000 pesos (12,000 yen) so I want to go back to that factory. Of course, I can trust my wife to take care of the family while I am gone.'

His thirty-six-year-old wife, Dolores, sat beside him in silence, nursing a baby. I asked her what she thought about her husband migrating. She said: 'I feel a great pain because I know how hard the work is, but we have to sacrifice ourselves to realize our dreams,' adding softly, 'if it were possible, of course, I don't want him to go; it's so lonely.'

Social worker Sister Noera said:

> Loneliness – this is the most serious problem. A migrant worker's wife, whose husband has left again after spending a holiday at home, does not wash her husband's clothes but hugs them to her for many days just like a child would do.

All the wives whom I visited spoke of their loneliness, and said that their only comfort was writing letters. 'I write letters two or three times a week. I have no more to write about,' said one sadly.

They also told me about the difficulty of bringing up children. 'It is not so easy to play the role of both mother and father.' If the period of a husband's migration extends to six or seven years, which is not uncommon, the responsibility of bringing up and educating the children rests solely on the wife's shoulders. 'Sometimes I have to counsel wives on the problems of juvenile delinquency,' said a worried-looking Mr Mon. Another problem is conflict with their mothers-in-law. 'Sometimes they have problems using the money their husbands send. Because they've had little experience with such comparatively large sums they don't know how to spend it and some simply waste it.' Mr Mon pointed out that these wives pay a high price in emotional terms in order to improve their living conditions.

Another noticeable thing was that most of the shiny new stereos, TV sets, refrigerators and so forth, placed in the centre of the small rooms in the slums were 'Made in Japan'. They were acquired at the expense of sweat and labour of migrant male workers and the humiliation of female migrant workers, in foreign countries, and of the pain of separation from those family members left behind.

Japan cannot, therefore, neglect the issue of overseas migration as something that is of no concern to that country. 'Is it because of the Philippine government's economic policy that so many families cannot live together in their own country? Do the Japanese people know that their government and corporations are supporting such a policy?' asked Mr Mon. I had to think again about this virtually invisible but firm link between the so-called 'manpower export' in the Philippines and Japan.

Pakistan

Migration policies are not limited to the Philippines; it is a common problem shared by most of the developing nations. In Karachi, Pakistan, I met woman journalist Nargis Ratiff, who was writing about this problem. According to her, 150,000 people leave Pakistan every year, and migrant workers now number over one million. When I visited the slums near Karachi port, here and there I noticed newly built and freshly painted houses. 'These are the homes of the "migrant rich",' Nargis told me. 'But in those houses the wives are suffering from "Dubai Syndrome".' This is a neurotic condition affecting women whose husbands are working in Dubai and other Middle East countries.

In 'Torn Families – The Women Suffer the Most', Nargis described the problems of migrants' wives who are left at home. One of them Gopi, whose husband was in Amman, Jordan, as a petroleum worker, lives with her children in her husband's family house. 'Since we must provide dowries for our daughters, and also support my three younger sisters who are married but not very well off, my husband has to endure such hard labour. I also help my mother-in-law who is a sweeper.' ('Sweeper' is a common job for the poor, a particular caste, who sweep houses, streets and buildings.) Gopi always worries about her husband and waits wearily for him to return home.

Fatima's husband has been working away for nine years. As an office worker, he used to earn only 500 rupees (9,000 yen) a month, but working in the Middle East he can now earn as much as 10,000 rupees a month. With the money he has sent home she has luxuriously redecorated her house, but she is frequently sick and has twice undergone surgery. Fatima's mother visits her from time to time, and cries to see her daughter's lonely life. 'I feel so empty; my husband is absent for so long. My daughter is so fond of her father, and each time he leaves, she cries all day,' said Fatima, tearfully.

Nashira has three children and her journalist husband works in Kuwait. His job is insecure, however, so he comes and goes. 'I often get so depressed, but I say to myself that I have to feed, educate, and give some joy to my children. My only comfort is my daughter who is very kind to me. Without her, I don't know what might have happened to me,' Nashira told me.

Gopi, Fatima, Nashira are ordinary migrants' wives to be found anywhere in Pakistan, whose loneliness is common to all women in those developing countries that export manpower.

I will never forget a scene at the airport in Chittagong, the second largest city in Bangladesh. While waiting for a flight to Dhaka, I happened to notice a big crowd of women dressed in variously coloured saris. Some carried babies; some held young children by the hand; all of them were desperately waving handkerchiefs or the end of their saris. Their eyes were focused intently on the plane that was taking off. Some of the women were shouting something. They were seeing off their husbands who were leaving to work in foreign countries. Only after the plane disappeared into the sky did the women begin to leave. These wives will endure their husbands' absence for many years.

Increasing overseas migration

As long as the problem of low wages and high unemployment is not solved in their home countries millions of workers, men and women, will continue to migrate to the developed and Middle East countries. There, they are abused, insulted, exploited, and discriminated against as workers of the lowest ranks at the bottom stratum of the society in the countries where they work. Each one of these workers worries about the family from which s/he is separated. Today, at this moment, they are working in sweat and tears in strange, far-away countries, dreaming of the day when they can join their families in their home countries free from such worries.

As a result of the development of technology in aviation and communication, and the scale of multinationalization of industries, overseas migration is expanding globally. The labour and sex of poor people in poor countries are being bought and sold as commodities.

Seeking solutions to this modern slavery, which takes the form of violations of migrant workers' human rights, there have been many conferences, including some specifically concerned with women. In autumn 1984, there was a 'Consultation on Migrant Women' held in Manila, and in December 1985, an 'Asian Migration Research Conference' was held in Hong Kong; in July 1985, at the Nairobi Conference of the UN Women's Decade, a number of workshops addressed this issue.

At all of these conferences it was recognized that without a structural change in the global economic system within the North–South framework, no solution of the problems of overseas migration was possible. At the same time, various measures to alleviate violations of migrant workers' human rights were discussed as a first priority: prevention of kick-backs by migrant workers' agents, low wages and non-payment of wages, inhuman working conditions, forced remittance of salary to the home country, and so on. The second task would be to organize a migrant workers union, and the third, to take joint action in an international network of those concerned about this issue.

'Migrant workers are selling their labour but not their human rights or human dignity,' was a comment made at the Hong Kong conference. Japanese women – and others – should be aware of the problems of Asian women working in foreign countries as domestic servants or entertainers, and participate in international actions.

We are leaving home.
Oh, how our hearts ache,
Tears well in our eyes,
There stand our children,
Seeing us off.
How we will miss them.

When will we see you again?
We'll be gone . . . but not forever.
Goodbye brothers . . . we'll be back

We go to work . . .
Away from home.
Hard work we fear not,
We toil for Thailand.

Though we live far away,
Our hearts stay home,
Thousands of miles from Thailand.
Those whom we leave behind
Will always be on our minds
We miss Thailand . . . we miss Thailand.

Chitrnath Vajarasathien
Dedicated to Thai workers in Saudi Arabia

5.
Sexual Exploitation of Women: Child Prostitution and the Expanding Sex Industry

Introduction

Phuket Island, southern Thailand's newly developed tourist resort, one of Asia's most beautiful beaches widely advertised as 'Paradise', became Hell in late January 1984 when a fire destroyed a brothel there, and the burned bodies of five young girls were found in the locked basement ruins. The ages of these five girls ranged from nine to twelve years; two of them were sisters. When I heard the news I remembered the innocent smiles on the faces of many young Thai girls whom I had seen in various red-light districts.

Shocked by this tragedy, Professor Rutnin Mattani, of Thammasat University's drama department, Bangkok, produced a video film on child prostitution, *Tomorrow Will There Be a Rainbow?* At the opening preview in April 1984, Professor Mattani made this appeal, 'Today is Good Friday. Please view this film with prayers for these five young girls who bore such heavy crosses during their short lives, that they might have a new life in heaven.' Because she is a Christian Rutnin Mattani added, 'My intention here is not to criticize Buddhism; we simply want to protect young girls' human rights.' This was to avoid any distortion of her reasons and purpose in showing this film in a Buddhist country, which might imply an anti-Buddhist or anti-Thai slant.

The video began with a scene of the fire showing the firemen unable to deal with the intense flames. Then the terrifying sight of five small bodies resembling lumps of charcoal laid on the ground. I could hardly bear to look: small, stiff, blackened arms reaching out as if for help.

The camera shifted to scenes of Chiang Mai, Chiang Rai, Payao, Lampoon – poverty-stricken areas in northern Thailand known as suppliers of prostitutes. The two sisters killed in the fire were born in a village in Chiang Rai in the most northern district. Professor Mattani had finally managed to locate their home, a primitive, bare hut. The parents appeared to be typical peasants, their faces expressionless, perhaps due to shock. The mother, speaking in a low voice said, 'We have ten children and cannot feed them all. We had to send them to town; there was no other way.' The toothless, tired-faced father stares wordlessly at the camera and then lowers his eyes.

The camera then closes in on the face of the seven-year-old sister of the two dead girls and the narrator says, 'After losing two breadwinners, what will happen to this family? Will she be the next one to be sold?' This child, dressed in rags, turns a shy and innocent smile towards the camera. She is probably unaware of her elder sisters' death, and has no idea of what her own future will be.

The camera then cuts to a splendid seven-storey monastery in Chiang Rai. In an interview the orange-robed abbot spoke in a voice devoid of emotion. 'Yes, of course there were also some offerings received from these girls; they hope for happiness in the next life.' For these young girls, life in this world is so miserable and hard that they must seek happiness in another. From the little they receive from selling their bodies, they give back some for this purpose. What kind of religion is this that can receive such offerings so insensitively, and build gorgeous temples at the expense of these young girls?

Thailand is a Buddhist country, with an estimated 300,000 monks, while, according to Thai police figures, there are 700,000 prostitutes throughout the country. 'Thailand, the land of smiles, has become the brothel of Asia.' 'The prostitute, wearing a pendant necklace of the image of Buddha, serves her customer with a smile,' and so on. The media is featuring reports on this situation; they are concerned not only for the tragedy of the women, but also for the bad image of the country. Thailand is proud of its long history and rich culture, but prostitution is becoming a big social problem.

Particularly disturbing is the fact that the age of the prostitutes is getting lower and lower. Professor Mattani says that ten percent are now under fourteen years of age. In spring 1984, around one hundred prostitutes were taken into 'protective custody' by Bangkok police. Nearly all of them were thirteen- to fourteen-year-olds. To force a young girl into prostitution is to practise slavery, and a violation of human rights. Child prostitution is increasing in every Asian country, and since it is profitable, competition is high among those involved in it. Therefore, the young, fresh, easy-to-control, early teenage girls become a much sought-after commodity. The brothel fire on Phuket Island, and the consequent deaths of the young girl prostitutes, illustrates the reality of the extent of sexual exploitation of children.

Visit to a Bangkok 'teahouse'

Yaowarat, in Bangkok's Chinatown, is a centre for child prostitution. The brothels are called 'teahouses', and there are about fifty of them located in this area. I asked a Thai man who had studied in Japan to escort me there, as I had been told that this was a dangerous place. On a door facing the street 'Teahouse' was inscribed in Chinese characters. As we opened the door, a threatening voice yelled from upstairs, 'No women allowed. Go away.' We tried another teahouse across the street. This time we entered and ran up the back stairs. We came upon more than ten girls – some looked very young – seated on a bench in the hallway, each with a number pinned to her chest.

A Chinese man, probably the owner of the place, appeared and began to argue with my escort in the Thai language. Meanwhile, the middle-aged madam, curious about this Japanese woman who had suddenly barged in, said to me in English, 'We have Japanese men here but we have never had a Japanese woman before!' I had been told that the teahouses are used only by local Thai men rather than tourists but, to my surprise, I discovered that Japanese men seek sex objects even in such places as this. The woman continued, 'The young Japanese men who stay in cheap hotels around here use this place.'

As the two men continued to argue, the woman invited me to look behind a small door, 'Just take a peek, but no pictures.' The narrow corridor was dark and I could see small toilet-sized rooms on either side, each about two metres square, just large enough to accommodate a bed. Through the half-opened door of one of these rooms I could see a man lying on the bed, dressed only in his underpants, and the back of the slender shoulder of a small girl. In such surroundings, devoid of light and suffocatingly close, young girls' bodies are used for the pleasure of men. As we left, we again passed by the young girls seated on the bench waiting for customers. I felt such pain, I was unable to meet their gaze.

The poorest and most depressed agricultural areas are in north and north-eastern Thailand and are reputed to have beautiful young girls, a result of intermarriage among the hill tribes there. These girls are sold for about 5,000 baht (50,000 yen) to 10,000 baht, depending on their appearance. Since their parents have received the sale money in advance, the girls receive only about 5 baht per day (50 yen), serving three or four customers on a normal day, and ten on a holiday.

Noi, a fifteen-year-old tribal girl from the north, was picked up by the Thai police and brought to Bangkok Emergency Home, a private women's shelter established by Khunying Kanitha Wichiencharoen.

Noi told me about her life that was filled with fear and humiliation. 'The first night I was terrified. I cried and begged the teahouse owner to release me and he beat me. Then a fat Chinese man entered the room. I don't want to recall his face but I can't forget it.' Then thirteen-year-old Noi was purchased by this fat Chinese man for 5,000 baht.

In Bangkok, during the Chinese New Year, young virgin girls who have not yet menstruated bring a very high price. There is a Chinese belief that having sex with a young girl will enable a man to become younger. Noi's second customer paid 3,000 baht; the third, 500. The price drops sharply each time until she can be had for only eighty baht, the usual price.

Since the parents have already been paid, the flesh merchants would have nothing if the girls ran away; this is why they must be kept locked in. Even if these country girls were permitted to go out, they would be lost and frightened in a big urban jungle like Bangkok. Now fifteen years old, Noi knows nothing of the city; she has never been out of the teahouse. She was fed birth control pills every day and had no holidays, even during her menses. She was beaten if she refused to take a customer even when she was sick, and she eventually contracted venereal disease. During her two years in the teahouse, it is estimated that she served around 2,000 customers. She arrived at the shelter completely ravaged in both mind and body. The director of the Emergency Home, Khunying Kanitha, spoke with compassion. 'After she regains some of her health and rests here awhile, I would like to find her a job as a housemaid. Even if she returns to her village home, there will not be enough food for her.' Noi's plight is the same for thousands of young prostitutes in Thailand.

In this same city, Bangkok, there is an internationally known red-light district, Patpong Street; also known to Japanese. It began as a Rest and Recreation (R&R) centre for American servicemen during the Vietnam War, and now it is a flourishing tourist attraction. Promoted by the Thai government, tourism is the second highest foreign exchange earner for Thailand, and Patpong is a symbol of an expanding Thai tourist industry.

Bars and nightclubs line the streets, and as the doors swing open there are bursts of raucous music, and glimpses of colourful lights and nearly nude gogo dancers. Heavily made-up massage girls, each wearing a large number tag, are seated behind a glass window. This is a typical scene at huge massage parlours and is called a 'fish pond', or 'fish tank'. Usually, the women working in this area are older than the teahouse child prostitutes in Chinatown. Even so, they are still in their teens. They have more freedom to go out and some make a fair amount of money, as this is a famous prostitution area for tourists from Japan and the West.

Empower group

In February 1986, I visited Chantawipa Apisuk, founder of Empower, whose office is located near Patpong Street. She studied sociology at Thammasat University and then continued her studies in the United States. There she participated in the protests against the Vietnam War and later, in the women's liberation movement. On her return to Thailand in 1982, she decided to devote herself to issues of concern to Thai women. In 1985, through her associations with Patpong women, she established Empower, which aims to support women's efforts to become self-reliant, and help them realize alternative employment. Chantawipa explained why Empower started its 'Four P.M.' English class:

> If a woman can speak English she can avoid being cheated by foreign customers, and she will have more opportunity to promote herself from gogo dancer to waitress, which is a steady job with a fixed regular salary. In this way these girls may have better chances to learn skills and escape their dependence on the sex industry. . . . I want to be a friend rather than a teacher. Patpong girls want to be treated as human beings more than anything else.

Ranging in age from seventeen to twenty-six, over one hundred women now attend this English class. Some are married, some are unmarried mothers; all work at Patpong in the sex industry. 'I want them to recover their self-respect by their own power; to try and improve their working conditions, and find a new life in the future,' Chantawipa said.

Recently, Empower began to publish *Patpong Newsletter*, and the *Bangkok Post* reported, 'Bar-girls publish their own newspaper.' More and more, these women have been able to transform themselves from passive victims of sexual exploitation into women who resist it. I was really impressed by Chantawipa's long and continuous efforts to help these women become strong and more self-reliant.

Sold as girls from the farming villages to Bangkok's sex industry, they start working at the teahouses in Chinatown – the lowest brothels at the bottom. Some of them move up to Patpong, gaining some freedom, independence and income along the way and, if they are lucky, they might even migrate overseas. In 1984, one of the women in Empower's English class went from Patpong to a legitimate job in Japan.

Migrant women prostitutes

I went to a young Thai woman's funeral at one of the largest funeral halls in Hamburg, West Germany. Only twenty years old, she committed suicide by jumping from her eighth-floor apartment. She had been married to a German sailor whom she met in a Bangkok bar, and went to live in West Germany. But, her husband was a pimp and forced her into prostitution to earn extra money. When she met another man who offered her a better and more secure life, and helped her to get out of prostitution, she divorced her husband and married this man. He required that she be a good wife and restricted her freedom so that she was unable to earn extra money to send to her poor family in Thailand. This was a tragedy of an unfortunate woman who had to make a hard choice between the two roles of Eve [prostitute] and Mary [pure mother].

This tragic example of the death of a migrant woman was reported in an American magazine by Siriporn Skrobanek, Director of the Women's Information Center in Bangkok. After graduation from Chulalongkorn University in Bangkok, she earned a Master's degree at the Institute of Social Studies in the Netherlands with a dissertation on prostitution.

In October 1981, she joined the campaign against sex tourism and demonstrated with other women when the then Prime Minister Suzuki of Japan was visiting ASEAN countries; this led to her involvement in the prostitution issue. She was also inspired by the joint efforts of Japanese and Filipino women in the struggle against sex tourism. By 1986 she had established a centre in a three-storey building and her work there is supported by Western non-governmental organizations.

Siriporn works as a resource person for various conferences in Asia related to the subject of prostitution, and has attended many international meetings on women's issues. Her sharp intelligence masked by her gentle smile, she is to all appearances a typical Thai woman. But, once she speaks, she is a forceful advocate for women's rights and for the independence of prostitutes. At present her efforts are aimed particularly at two types of migrant Thai women: as she expresses it, 'One is the prostitute Eve; the other is the bride Mary.' Two types of women; two kinds of problems.

> In Thailand there are too many prostitutes and the competition is fierce. It is very difficult to earn enough money to support a large family. More and more women want to travel overseas to earn a higher income; they want to go to the developed countries where the standard of living is higher. They generally do this by making contact with a sex-tour customer, or contract for marriage with a catalogue agent. Many women who follow this latter route become victims of sexual exploitation just like the young woman who committed suicide in West Germany.

Siriporn interviewed Thai women living in and near West Germany, and she thought it very important to inform women who were planning to migrate of the dangerous pitfalls ahead. The centre also has many cases of women seeking counselling on other issues as well; for example, problems of rape, pornography, family violence – any form of behaviour or activity that dehumanizes women.

The structure of Thai prostitution is very complicated. It begins with children in the teahouses, expands to Patpong Street, Pattaya Beach, and Phuket Island, then overseas. In order to deal with the problems generated by these types of prostitution different kinds of support systems are needed. Khunying Kanitha's Emergency Home, Chantawipa's Empower group, and Siriporn's Women's Information Center are all actively involved in addressing these problems.

The patterns of structural economic dependence forced on developing countries result in impoverishment in agricultural communities. Peasant families are, in turn, forced into traditional patriarchal patterns of sacrificing their daughters to provide for large families. These two factors, combined with a growing tourist industry, have caused an explosive increase in prostitution. Women born into these poverty-stricken families have few alternatives. They either become low-wage or informal sector workers such as street vendors, or work in the sex industry within the country or abroad.

> Parents sell their daughters to an agent; the agent makes huge profits and pays off the police. Everyone knows this. Child prostitution is against the law but trafficking in young girls is widely practised. The agent is never prosecuted and the girl is the one who is punished.

Thus lecturer Teeranat Karnjanaukson of Chulalongkorn University criticizes those who profit from child prostitution. A member of Friends of Women, she helped organize the Anti-Trafficking Women Week campaign as part of the International Women's Day observance after the Phuket Island fire.

The women activists, lawyers, teachers, doctors, farmers – all those involved in this campaign, produced a statement saying:

> We should do away with the present anti-prostitution law that punishes only the victim; we should enforce the criminal law that prohibits anyone from forcing persons under eighteen years of age into prostitution; and we should punish the agents that violate these laws.

Today in Thailand, more and more voices are being raised against punishment of prostitutes and for decriminalization.

> An anti-prostitution law cannot change overnight the situation of thousands of women working in the sex industry. It is obvious that the political and economic system must be changed, but this will take a long time. We cannot wait. Our urgent task is to give these women day-to-day support so that they can do their business without police interference and survive.

This point has been made for years by the woman journalist Sukanya Hantrakul. It has now become the consensus of activists in the women's liberation movement who are dealing with the issue of prostitution in Thailand.

It seems to me that the reasoning behind this consensus is that there is little possibility of immediate structural change in Thai society. The people's movement for democracy that began with the student revolution in 1973 lasted only three years, and was brutally suppressed by the Thai army in 1976 on what has become known as Bloody Wednesday.

Sex tourism in the Philippines

Prostitution is a big social problem in the Philippines as well as in Thailand. Philippine women are as severely sexually exploited as Thai women, but there is clearly one major difference. In the Philippines, the problem of prostitution is taken up in the struggle to change an entire social structure, whereas in Thailand, it is seen as a problem for the women. This difference is even clearer in the light of the fact that the people's power movement for national liberation in the Philippines was strong enough to topple the Marcos dictatorship.

Prostitution in the Philippines takes forms surprisingly similar to that of Thailand: child prostitution, sex tourism, mail-order brides, and so forth. Under Marcos, promotion of tourism resulted in Manila's competing with Bangkok for the title of 'International Sex City'; Manila's reputation has become well-known, particularly to the Japanese.

Manila's Mabini area is similar to Bangkok's Patpong, with clubs and bars lining the streets, places to buy and sell sex, 'hospitality girls' with typically friendly Filipina smiles waiting for customers. Hotels near the Mabini area are full of women who cater to tourists from Japan and other countries. This is the same Mabini area where the first campaign meeting to protest against sex tourism in Asia was held in the St Paul Women's College auditorium in 1981, when former Japanese Prime Minister Suzuki visited Manila.

In September 1980, I attended the International Workshop on Tourism sponsored by the Christian Conference of Asia, and I had a chance to do some investigation on Japanese male tourists and sex tours at the Ramada Hotel, located just in front of the college.

I was shocked by the results. There were 600 rooms in this hotel and as many as 334 local women stayed overnight. Most of the guests were Japanese tour-group males visiting Manila during a holiday period. I stayed in the same hotel overnight and interviewed some of the 'hospitality girls' before they left the next morning. I also visited the house near the hotel where these girls stay; most of them were teenagers. They came from Visayas Islands, known as a very poor and economically depressed area, and from Tondo, the largest slum in Manila.

The women each receive about 100 pesos (US$5) for an overnight stay, which is only about ten percent of the amount paid by the customer ($60–$70). The oldest woman there was twenty-five years of age, a single mother of three children, who said to me, 'If I could get a regular job and make enough money to care for my children, I'd quit this work today.' Even though these women lose ninety percent of their sale price, they still make more money than a factory worker or a shop girl because the average wage level is extremely low.

Other things became clearer as I continued this research. For example, very little foreign money stays in the Philippines; most of it ultimately goes back to Japan. This is an exploitative structure on a national level. Japanese tourists are buying package tours from Japanese travel agencies, travelling on Japan Air Lines, staying at hotels owned by Japanese capital, enjoying sight-seeing tours arranged by Japanese travel agency branches, picking up women at Japanese-managed clubs, dining at Japanese restaurants, buying souvenirs at department stores backed by Japanese investments, and returning to Japan the same way they came – Japan Air Lines. This may seem an extreme case but I am simply describing this exploitative system. The conclusions reached at the International Workshop on Tourism in Manila put it quite plainly:

> It is only a myth that the developing countries benefit economically from tourism by earning foreign currency. Women are used as commodities within the North–South structure, and the rich countries become richer while the poor become poorer.

As I observe the exploitative structure of sex tourism, I see that it is not an individual moral problem, but an issue in North–South relations, and a problem of sex discrimination. I returned to Japan and reported my findings. This problem was also discussed in the Diet [national parliament], and the campaign against sex tourism gained strength. Responding to the Japanese movement, the Philippine women took action. The result was strong solidarity between Japanese women and Filipinas, culminating in a protest meeting attended by 1,000 women in Manila in January 1981. This meeting was also linked with protest action in Bangkok, which Siriporn Skrobanek of the Women's Information Center helped to organize.

The Philippine media also began to denounce Japanese sex tourists as 'military men in civilian clothes' – a reminder that the Philippines has been invaded by the Japanese Army in the past; now the same thing was happening in a different form – sex tourism and economic invasion. This sentiment was widely expressed in the Philippines and, as a result, the Japanese tourist agencies sent fewer travellers to Manila; by spring 1981, the number of Japanese tourists to Manila had decreased by twenty-five percent. But the economic structure that engenders prostitution remains the same, and those women who lost their jobs in the sex industry in Manila went to Japan as 'Japayuki' or became migrant workers in Western countries. (*Japayuki* literally means 'going to Japan'; it is a pejorative word applied to migrant women prostitutes coming into Japan.)

Japanese travel agents began to avoid 'sex city' – Manila – and developed new tourists resorts in other areas such as the Cebu Islands, which are covered by green coconut trees, surrounded by a shining blue ocean – and have lots of newly opened brothels. Within one or two years Cebu already had 'Japanese only' brothels. The expansion of overseas prostitution seen in the increasing numbers of migrant women, and the relocation of sex tours to various outlying areas are trends that can also be observed in Thailand.

Military-base prostitution

Military-base prostitution in Thailand faded away with the end of the Vietnam War, but it remains a serious problem in the Philippines today. Examples of a foreign military presence are the US Naval Base in Olongapo at Subic Bay, and Clark Air Force Base in Angeles. In autumn 1983, I visited Olongapo, located 110 kilometres north of Manila. It used to be a quiet fishing village and then became a flourishing R & R centre for US soldiers during the Vietnam War. Now it is home base for the US Seventh Fleet, with a population of 200,000 who depend on the sex industry and base employment for their livelihood.

Magsaysay Avenue is the main street leading to the base gate. It is lined on both sides with nightclubs, bars, discos, and money changers. There are over 300 R & R establishments employing 16,000 to 17,000 women. At one of these clubs, I saw about sixty semi-nude women, ranging in age from sixteen to thirty, dancing on a stage, but there were few customers as the Fleet had just sailed.

After she had finished her performance on stage, I talked with Betty, a twenty-year-old dancer and mother of two children. She told me that she comes from Visayas and gets 100 of the 300 pesos each customer pays for her 'service'. If she has no customers, she makes only twenty to thirty pesos a day from the sale of drinks. She is one of 6,000 licensed hostesses in Olongapo who are required to have a medical check for venereal disease every two weeks. She showed me her certificate.

The next morning I visited a clinic where about 500 women were seated on benches waiting to be examined. The city licenses its hostesses in order to service the sexual needs of US soldiers. Hoping to avoid venereal disease among its servicemen, the US government opened the first clinic here in 1970. This co-operation between the US and Philippine governments thereby supports the structure of military-base prostitution.

Dr Mariano, the woman director of the clinic I visited, said proudly, 'The American side feels strongly about keeping venereal disease under control, and we have kept the infectious rate to within three to four percent.' In the summer of 1982, however, there was a serious outbreak of venereal disease that hospitalized twelve girls between the ages of nine and fourteen. It was supposed to have been kept secret but the nuns who work in the hospital reported this incident to a local Irish priest. Because he was shocked by the blatant violation of the human rights of these young girls, and despite government pressure to desist, he made public a report on the facts of child prostitution in Olongapo.

Father Shay Cullen, who since 1969 has lived in Olongapo where he established a drug rehabilitation centre for young men addicts, said:

> These young girls from the slums and orphanages are forced into prostitution through a criminal syndicate. They receive from ten to sixty pesos for each customer. I could no longer keep silent when I see these children, victims of such inhuman treatment. I put their stories on tape and took pictures of them. The base commander pressured me not to disclose this situation, but I felt that I must do so, and through the mass media I made public charges against those who use these children so cruelly.

Because of his protest action that 'dishonoured' the city, this priest was asked to leave the country even though he had worked there for more than thirteen years. A campaign to 'protect Father Cullen', with support from both inside and outside the country, brought him a reprieve, and he was just barely permitted to remain. Because the demand for fresh young girls for prostitution purposes continues, this priest continues to protest against the violation of human rights to the US military authorities. He insists, 'This kind of prostitution should be called rape or sexual violence.'

Since the Vietnam War, Olongapo has become one of the most famous red-light districts in all of Asia, and the women who find their way here come from the poor agricultural areas of the Philippines. In a social studies survey, Professor Leopoldo Moselina of Colomba College in Olongapo, analysed the women's situation thus:

> [a] typical example of economic dependency determined by outside forces. They have no fixed salaries, no holidays, no social welfare, no right to organize themselves, and unstable employment. They are always facing dangerous health hazards such as venereal disease, abortion, and drug abuse; ultimately, they suffer social discrimination.
>
> They can work only until their mid-thirties; after that they

become maids or laundresses, or shop clerks, and, in the worst case, beggars – the bottom of the heap. If they have daughters, they put them in the prostitution business.

Their biggest dream is to marry an American serviceman but less than six percent do so, and the percentage of divorces among them is quite high. As a result, because of their poverty, they get caught up in the sex industry. Even if they leave they end up in poverty, and usually this poverty continues to the next generation. The problem is how to change this dehumanizing economic structure that exploits poor women, forcing them into dependency on the sex industry.

Professor Moselina's conclusions, based on his research, accurately describe the present situation and various forms of the expansion of prostitution in Asia. Sex tourism, international trafficking in women, child prostitution, military-base prostitution – all exist in both Thailand and the Philippines, and while the form and scale may differ, all are on the increase in most Asian, as well as other Third World countries.

Poverty, as a result of a development policy favouring the interests of First World countries, expanding tourism, militarization; patriarchal traditions that foster contempt for women, international/multinational trafficking of women due to advances in transport and communications are all factors that contribute to the exploitation and commoditization of countless Third World women. The unprecedented expansion of prostitution is a clear symptom of a sick society and, in social as in physical sickness, the cause, not just the symptom must be attacked. The campaign against sex tours has alerted women's awareness, but has, so far, failed to curb the expansion of prostitution in the Third World.

6.
Dowry and Rape: Women Against Traditional Discrimination

Dowry deaths

When, at a meeting on Asian women in 1980 in Kyoto, I heard the words 'dowry murder' for the first time in an Indian woman's speech, I was deeply shocked. According to her, if a bride's family fails to pay the amount of dowry demanded by the prospective groom's family, the bride will be cruelly treated by the in-laws, and in many cases will be burned to death in a paraffin fire, or forced to commit suicide. Such an unbelievable atrocity is not something that belongs to a primitive past, it is still rampant in India today.

The following year, 1981, during a visit to New Delhi, I was truly astounded to find the situation much more serious than I had imagined. At that time the anti-dowry struggle, along with the anti-rape campaigns, had become the most important objectives of the Indian women's movement.

'In the Delhi area alone, one dowry death is exposed every day. In order to fight against such a terrible custom, women's organizations are now sponsoring an anti-dowry exhibition. Please go and see it first.' So Pramila Dandavate, who, as Congresswoman had been working with such issues for many years, advised me as a visitor from a far country. It is true that 'seeing is believing'.

Among the photographs in the Anti-dowry Exhibition at Parliament House was one of a family weeping and mourning as they gathered around their daughter's charred remains. Another photograph showed a woman's burned body with arms outstretched as if pleading for help. I had to look away from the next one that showed the victim's burned face with the teeth as the only recognizable part. Beside each gruesome picture of the victim was a photograph of the same woman when she was alive, smiling, young and beautiful. What agonies they must have suffered as their short lives ended in the flames.

In one section of the exhibition, anti-dowry posters were displayed.

One showed a sari-clad woman crying out from the midst of the flames that engulfed her; another showed a woman trying to cut away the chains that bound her. These posters vividly communicated the humiliation of the woman, and also aroused the desire to protest against such unbelievable ill-treatment.

Another part of the exhibition displayed photographs of the anti-dowry demonstrations. One showed a group of women carrying an effigy of a man who had burned his wife to death; they were marching near his home. Clenching their fists high, with mouths open wide to shout, they expressed their outrage and appealed for an end to such savagery.

Two years later, when I visited the Citizens Documentation Centre in Bombay, I was surprised to find a thick file containing a collection of newspaper and magazines articles reporting dowry murders. Inside was page after page of photographs of women who had burned to death, each accompanied by its counterpart, showing the young woman's smiling face in life. I discovered that dowry deaths occurred not only in the New Delhi area, but throughout the country, and they are increasing. Every one of the articles told a similar story, and I was stunned to think of the terrible torture each one of these women victims had suffered.

One example is Kanchan Mala Hardy, nineteen years old at the time of her death. Kanchan met Sunil Hardy, four years her senior, when they were both college students; they were married in 1979. Her parents provided clothes, jewellery, and household goods worth 20,000 rupees (46,000 yen) as dowry, but were unable to give the refrigerator, TV set, and 10,000 rupees more demanded by the groom's family. Trouble began barely two months after the wedding. Kanchan's husband began to ill-treat her. When he beat her with a belt she returned to her family's home because of his continuing and increasingly violent behaviour towards her. She took a job to support herself, but three days after she started working, her husband came and persuaded her to return to him and celebrate their first wedding anniversary. A few days later, Kanchan's mother was informed, 'Kanchan's hands are slightly burned and she has been hospitalized.' The mother rushed to the hospital only to find that her daughter was dead. A policeman asked her if she knew of anyone who might have cause to harm her daughter; she mentioned the dowry demand. Then she was taken to see Kanchan's terribly burned body and was deeply shocked. 'It didn't look like my daughter. I couldn't believe it was my daughter.'

Some time later, Kanchan's family received an anonymous letter from a neighbour of the Hardy family saying, 'Maybe she wouldn't have died if you had given a TV set.' Another letter from a different neighbour said:

> Kanchan had been screaming for ten minutes before her mother-in-law allowed someone to go in and rescue her. Neighbours banging on the door and looking through a window saw the mother-in-law changing her clothes and Sunil Hardy drinking a glass of milk while Kanchan was burning to death. Kanchan's mother-in-law was always shouting at her for having come without a TV set.

The first photograph I had seen at the Delhi exhibition was of Kanchan's mother and sisters crying over her charred body. Although Kanchan's husband and mother-in-law were prosecuted they were finally released on the grounds of insufficient evidence. Sunil has since remarried, but Kanchan's mother committed suicide and the deeply grieving father, having lost both his daughter and his wife, made no further appeal for justice.

Kanchan is only one of hundreds of thousands of victimized women who have perished in this horrible way. Because dowry murder is a crime committed behind the closed doors of a private home and it is very difficult to find witnesses it is commonly camouflaged as suicide. Very often, policemen who are called to the scene of such tragedies are easily persuaded that the cause of death was suicide; and, as is well known, the payment of bribes frequently then takes place. There are, in fact, cases of suicide by brides, as a result of ill-treatment at the hands of husbands and in-laws, and some desperate young women are even forced into burning themselves.

On 8 June 1983, in New Delhi, a woman student who had recently married, taking a dowry of 50,000 rupees, burned to death only three months after the ceremony. Her family had been asked to provide a motorbike as part of her dowry, and when it was not forthcoming the bride was badly beaten. During the eight-day period following this incident, sixteen women were reported to have perished in flames. In the same year, in Bihar state, in north-east India, there was reported the burning of eighteen-year-old Mina, murdered by her father-in-law and other relatives also for having failed to provide a motorbike with her dowry. During the following three months, nine women in the rural area of this state were killed in similar circumstances.

How many cases of dowry death are there in India? Statistics compiled from the New Delhi area alone show that in 1970 there were about 300 dowry deaths; in 1982 and 1983, this number had more than doubled. It is estimated that throughout the country there are several thousand dowry deaths each year.

New Delhi Congresswoman Dandavate said,

> Dowry used to be a custom practised mainly among wealthy Hindu families only, but now it has expanded to Muslims, Christians, and the common people in the rural areas, and even to the tribal people; it is a social issue in the entire nation.

And the situation worsens.

The yoke of tradition

The history of the dowry system is at least as old as the caste system in India. Hindu scriptures say that the giving of a daughter in marriage carries a religious symbolism for the parents. It is a kind of alms-giving, and when the bride is handed over to the bridegroom, he must be given something in cash or kind to reward him for his willingness to receive the woman. The ancient Hindu Manu scripture, thought to be the origin of the custom of dowry, states: 'No marriage is complete unless the woman is given different kinds of gifts such as clothing, jewellery, and so forth, at the time of the marriage.'

Such a concept of marriage is based on a discriminatory concept of women. That is, women are merely objects to be given away, or useless goods, even a burden; they have to be disposed of by paying a dowry. In other words, women are property to be transferred between their fathers and their husbands, and the dowry is a calculation of a bride's monetary worth.

> In India, we have a glorious heritage of systematic violence toward women within the family itself. *Sati*, the custom of self-immolation in which the wife is burned alive on the funeral pyre of her husband, and female infanticide, are the two better-known forms. Today, we do not kill girl babies at birth; we let them die through systematic neglect. The mortality rate among female children is thirty to sixty percent higher than among male children. Today, we do not wait until a woman is widowed before we burn her to death. We burn her during the lifetime of her husband so that he can get a new bride with a fatter dowry.

This extract from *Manushi*, a feminist magazine widely read both inside and outside India, pointedly exposes and bitterly criticizes the heavy yoke of traditional sex discrimination that Indian women have to bear.

I visited Nalini Singh, author of a lengthy article, 'Why Dowry Spells Death', for the newspaper *Indian Express*, in 1981; she herself is a modern woman having studied abroad in the United States. She became interested in the dowry issue after talking with parents whose daughters had burned to death. Her critique of the Indian concept of women is sharp and profound:

> Dowry is the product of an ideology that one's gender determines one's worth or significance. Society perceives women as economically less productive than men, and, therefore, a female is regarded as a net economic drain on a family. At the time of marriage, when the female is in transit between the two households, the family that accepts her is perceived to be saddled with a new economic liability, and the household that is losing her is, in fact, losing a liability. The dowry then becomes a compensatory payment to the family that agrees to shelter her. Even if the bride brings a salary, she is regarded as a *de facto* burden, and she has also to bring a dowry because she is female. Consequently, men attach great importance to a dowry as a means of displaying their wealth, power, and status, and retaliate against women who do not submit to their authority or comply with the system that gives them this authority, by burning them to death. Women cannot return to their own parents' home, and they can find no place for themselves. As a result they suffer loss of dignity, self-esteem, and hope for the future, which forces them to commit suicide.

The tragedy is that there is no escape for women from such situations; economic independence is still very difficult, and social pressure against divorce still very strong.

Dowry and consumer culture

Since the dowry's origin is so ancient, why has its practice increased on such a scale that by the 1970s it had become a social evil? It is probably due to the cult of materialism, which, as a result of modernization, economic development, and a consumer culture that envelops the whole Indian society, is now widely acceptable. The value of human beings is now measured by the wealth they possess; and the amount of dowry provided is seen as a reflection of the social status of the bride's family. In this social climate demands by a woman's prospective in-laws are, therefore, escalating.

> In former times, the dowry consisted only of clothing and jewellery for the bride, and some household articles, but now the in-law family demands cash, electronic products, and even expenses for overseas travel. The average annual salary for a government official is just 1,000 rupees; a daughter's dowry will be from 30,000 to 40,000 rupees. This is why so many people borrow from their retirement allowance, and are repaying the debt by taking out loans. As a result, dowry causes corruption among government officials. When a baby girl is born her whole family is unhappy because they are worried about the dowry for this newborn daughter.

Thus did Shanti Shacrabati deplore the dowry issue when I interviewed her on the situation regarding rural women. She had organized more than 60,000 groups of women from all around the country, and they have pledged not to pay dowries, because this is a root cause of agony for young brides in rural villages too. For example, in one tribal group, the rate for a dowry used to be ten to twenty rupees until around the mid-1930s; now the top price is 1,000 rupees.

Most of the dowry tragedies occur in the urban lower middle class, which is having a difficult time economically, and continues to be unstable in a rapidly changing society. A survey of thirty-three cases of dowry deaths in New Delhi during the first half of 1983 reveals that two-thirds of the victims' husbands were from families without regular incomes. For example: a railway station bookseller; food salesman; self-employed mechanic; car driver; butcher; pen manufacturer; daily-employed factory worker; part-time staff of an anti-malaria bureau. Most of them had migrated from rural areas and lived in newly developed areas where housing was too crowded to allow for large, extended families. Such families want to maintain a certain level of lifestyle but have unstable incomes; they thus tend to depend on the bride's parents to provide a generous dowry. Women who marry into families who are economically worse off than their own have to adapt themselves to a less comfortable life. They are also under extreme pressure from their in-laws' dowry demands and finally they very often resort to suicide.

The dowry issue has another, different aspect that also is quite important. Daughters of poor families, which are unable to provide dowries, cannot hope to marry; and families without sons pay dowries for their daughters but receive nothing to make up for this loss. This places some families in a very real difficulty.

> We are ten sisters and none of us is married yet. Our father is poor but in our area young unmarried women are not allowed to work in someone else's family to get income. We are middle school graduates but we have to stay at home. We wonder what will happen to us in the future.

> My daughter has graduated from university with very good marks, but we have no money for her dowry. The family that wants her are very good people and ask us to pay only for the wedding ceremony and the banquet, but we cannot even afford that. Because we cannot pay a dowry, we cannot marry off our daughter.

These difficulties were explained to Jamila Verghese, who has written a book on dowry murder. Thus not only married women suffer under the dowry system. Those unmarried women for whom a dowry cannot be provided also suffer because they can have no hope of marriage. Parents who pay a dowry for their daughter hope to compensate by receiving one when their sons marry. It is not easy to break out of this truly vicious circle.

It is a dreadful irony to see so many advertisements in newspapers and in magazines such as: 'University man [of a certain age] wants to marry a woman [of a certain age]. The dowry is a few thousand rupees . . .' appearing in the same newspaper that reports a dowry murder.

Anti-dowry movements

Because of such situations, the anti-dowry movement has been vigorously and persistently pursued in India. It is, of course, women who have been organizing the struggles. The 1975 death by burning of a woman in New Delhi named Omwati sparked the first anti-dowry demonstration and, since then, the dowry issue has been one of the most important common targets of the Indian women's movement.

I visited Sarla Mudgal, who had organized this first demonstration. 'We have been struggling against the tradition of dowry with all our might. It will take another ten to twenty years to solve the problem, but we are determined to continue our struggle until no woman will ever again be victimized in this way,' she said. Formerly Sarla Mudgal had worked in social welfare activities such as rescuing prostitutes, helping with the remarriage of widows, and providing shelters for abandoned women. But in the 1970s, as the dowry issue became more serious she turned her attention to this problem. Of the 300 to 400 cases that her group has dealt with, there were 150 dowry deaths.

Supported by about 300 members of her group, Sarla Mudgal was promoting vigorous campaign actions such as a witness rally of the parents of those women who had been burned to death, and a hunger strike in front of the Ministry of Home Education. This was the group pictured in the New Delhi exhibition mentioned earlier that demonstrated against a man accused of burning his wife to death; they carried his effigy for all to see. They are also active in support of justice in the courts for the victims of dowry murder, and they arrange family meetings for educational purposes and general understanding of the issue.

The anti-dowry movement was spreading from New Delhi all over the country. Every time a dowry death occurred, women in that area took action. Efforts were made to prosecute the persons responsible for the murder of the bride. Police treat ninety percent of unnatural deaths related to dowry as accidents, five percent are considered to be suicide; the remaining five percent are suspected murder. This being the case, once a death is reported, the women investigate to ascertain the truth. Otherwise, these cases might be completely concealed. Even when they succeed in bringing the case to court, the murderer is usually set free on grounds of insufficient evidence.

Under such circumstances, history was made in May 1983 when the judge of the New Delhi District Court, Mr S. M. Aggarwal, pronounced the death sentence on three culprits convicted in a bride-burning case. This crime took place in 1980 when a young wife, Suda, who was expecting the birth of her baby within a few days, was burned to death by her husband, brother- and mother-in-law in a petrol fire. In November 1983, however, the High Court dismissed this unusual sentence on the grounds of insufficient evidence, and the three were set free. Those guilty of bride-burning are not punished – a state of affairs that continues to this day.

The Prohibition of Dowry Act was passed in 1961, but found to be ineffective because even though it deems payment of a dowry unlawful, it does not rule out gifts, neither does it draw a distinction between the two. Congresswoman Dandavate organized seminars, and women's organizations continued to lobby on this issue and, in

1980, the government was forced to set up a joint committee from both houses of Parliament to consider an amendment to this Act. Finally, in 1984, an amendment was passed determining that gifts of excessive value given at the time of marriage are considered to be unlawful dowry. In addition, not only the parents of a victim, but also interested third parties, such as welfare agencies or women's organizations, may file a complaint if the victim's parents are not willing to take legal action. This amendment is certainly progress, but because it continues to provide legal loopholes, it, too, lacks the means to abolish this evil custom.

Some progress has also been made with the provision of an amendment to the criminal law in cases of dowry deaths. According to this amendment, cruelty in terms of mental and physical torture, and abetment by a woman's husband or his relatives in her suicide is punishable by imprisonment for up to three years, and liability to a fine. It also provides for a thorough police investigation in the event of a woman's death within seven years of her marriage, and the investigating police officer is empowered to order a post-mortem to be made in such cases. This improvement in the criminal law is also as a result of vigorous campaigning by women's organizations.

> We are fighting for better legislation on dowry but we must remember that, at the same time, we have to challenge the social attitudes towards women as a burden, a useless creature without any individuality. The assumption that a husband is given dowry to shoulder the burden of a wife needs to be questioned. Education in economic independence for women should be emphasized. Women need to have more self-confidence. There should be a total ban on dowry, and women should be given an effective share in property.

So exclaimed Vibhuti Patel of the Bombay Women's Centre at the Asian Women's Conference in Davao, Philippines. She emphasized the importance of changing social attitudes; simply changing laws is not enough to finally and effectively eliminate demands for dowry.

The conclusion is inescapable; dowry is a modern product of sexist ideology historically rooted in Indian society, and to struggle against dowry is to question such ideology.

Fighting against rape

Another important direction the women's liberation movement in

India takes is the anti-rape struggle. Rape is also a symptom of discrimination against women, deeply rooted in Indian society, and a serious social issue as well.

> When walking alone
> in the darkness
> identifying myself with
> the silent, serene mood of night,
>
> I feel
> an electric current
> passing through my limbs
> when the car swerves past
> and the lorry rushes by
> roaring . . .
>
> Oh, the dark night
> frightens me not
> but the sight of man
> makes me shrink

(C. G. Manjula)

When I visited New Delhi in the autumn of 1981, I was afraid to go out at night alone. This poem, 'Beast in Darkness', published in *Manushi*, was understandable to me. Many women in India told me that cases of rape were increasing rapidly, and the rapist, not uncommonly, may be a personal friend or relative of the victim. In March 1980, on International Women's Day, a countrywide anti-rape campaign was launched, largely in response to the Supreme Court's ruling on the controversial 'Mathura Case' in autumn 1979.

In March 1972, Mathura, a fifteen-year-old girl, who had been orphaned at an early age, was living with her brother in a village near Bombay. In the house where she was employed Mathura had met a young man and they wanted to marry, but her brother was opposed to this. He reported to the police that the young man and his family had kidnapped his underage sister. At 9 o'clock the same evening, Mathura and her brother and the young man and his family were called to the police station where three policemen took statements from the young couple. At this point, one policeman left to go home. Later as Mathura was about to leave the police station with the other people, one of the remaining policemen seized her by the arm and ordered her to follow him and told her brother and the others to leave. Mathura was dragged into the backyard and raped. As she lay on the ground, another policeman also tried to rape her but he was too drunk to do so.

Mathura's brother and the others were waiting outside, wondering what had happened when the drunken policeman came out and told them, 'Mathura has gone.' Shortly after that, Mathura crawled out of the station and told the people gathered there that she had been raped. She was taken to a doctor who, on hearing her story, advised her to report the matter to higher authorities. As the news of this incident began to spread throughout the neighbourhood, people gathered near the police station shouting, 'Beat the rapist policemen!' and 'Burn down the police station!'

When this case was brought to court, the District Court ruled that the policemen were not guilty because

> Mathura had already had sexual relations with her fiancé, her body had no lasting marks, and it was not forced but on consent. Therefore it was not rape. She made up the story that she had been raped in order to show her faithfulness to her fiancé.

The High Court reversed this decision and sentenced the policeman who had raped Mathura to five years' imprisonment and the policeman who had failed to rape but had abused her was sentenced to one year's imprisonment. The High Court's decision was premised on the grounds that consent and passive submission should be distinct, and that the circumstances indicated that it was forced sexual intercourse. But the Supreme Court reversed the High Court ruling and acquitted the two policemen because 'It cannot be considered as rape unless the woman is under threat of death or serious injury, but there is no evidence that Mathura resisted, and the sexual act was done peacefully.'

This Supreme Court judgement ignited the rage of women all over India because they found it unacceptable and that it completely ignored the human rights of women. The anti-rape campaign had begun.

As if encouraged by this judgement, rape cases in which the accused was a policeman increased drastically. For example, in the state of Uttar Pradesh alone as many as nineteen such rape cases were reported within three months from January 1980, and this was only the tip of the iceberg. The rapists are rarely found guilty while, on the other hand, the victimized women are accused of being 'immoral', or 'bad', or 'they consented', and the rapists go free.

Many of the rape victims are poor women in the 'untouchable' caste or tribal women. We can never forgive those rapists who take advantage of their power and violate women in the weakest social position. Therefore, we will never stop our anti-rape demonstrations, no matter what abuses we may suffer for it. Sometimes we even go to the rapists' homes to protest.

These are the defiant words of women activists in Bombay who formed an anti-rape forum in March 1980 who were moved to act by their deep anger and rage.

Figures from the Citizens Documentation Centre in Bombay show an increase in rape cases nationwide, especially among the 'untouchable' and tribal women, proving the activists' assertions. These figures, of course, include only reported cases; many incidents in the lower castes are not reported, as people who belong to these castes are not treated as human beings. The women, especially, are considered to be rubbish, and any mistreatment of them is acceptable. The contempt shown for other less powerful human beings is the root cause of these atrocities. The women victimized by sexual assault are seriously injured and humiliated due to class and gender discrimination. The men who rape women are not punished, while these victims are forced to leave their villages, often turning to prostitution or suicide in their despair. Reports of such painful cases are not unusual.

Women at the Bombay centre said that,

Rapists are not only policemen; men of power and in responsible positions, who are supposed to be protecting women, are often the attackers. It is really a hopeless situation. For example, there are so many incidents of rape on the trains that women cannot travel safely. This is why the women's movements had campaigns demanding that the railway authorities have security patrols assigned to the trains. This was finally accomplished and then it was the men on the patrols who committed the crimes against women travellers. We are waging an endless battle.

There are numerous documented stories: an untouchable caste woman was raped and killed by a staff member of a public hostel and the case was treated as a suicide; a nineteen-year-old woman, hospitalized for an ear operation, was raped during the night by a hospital cleaner, resulting in the young woman having mental problems, but the rapist escaped; a woman looking for a safe place to stay came to a shelter established for that purpose and was raped by a counsellor employed there. Even in prison, women are raped by guards. Women's magazines in India are full of such violent incidents, reported in every district in the country.

Frequently, rapists are those men at lower levels of the very power structures established to protect women, and the victims are women who are powerless; and, again, the rapists are not punished and the victims are condemned. The essence of rape is the assault of the weak by the strong in its most extreme form.

The anti-rape struggle by most of the women's movements has spread to the whole country. Women are questioning rape cases in local districts, and have campaigned for change in the existing laws governing such cases. This resulted in amendments to criminal laws in late 1983, which included changes related to punishment in rape cases. Notably, conviction for committing the crime of rape brings seven years' imprisonment, and in cases of multiple rape, rape by police officers, and rape of pregnant women, the penalty is ten years. In cases where the rapist is a man whose official position is one of responsibility for the protection of women, such as a policeman, a hospital staff member, a prison guard, and other such public service workers, the man is required to prove that the victim gave her consent if she has denied doing so.

In addition to the progressive judicial amendments described above, there are still some points of contention between the women's movements and the law: the provision that to identify the rape victim is unlawful makes the task of organizing public debate on individual cases and campaigns against specific rapists very difficult; marital rape was not considered; investigation of the sexual histories of women who are rape victims was not prohibited. Thus, the amendments fall short of the demands of feminist movements. As Vibhuti Patel from Bombay summed up the matter: 'These amendments to the laws concerning rape are insufficient and do not meet the aspirations of women's movements. We must continue our work towards the prevention of rape.'

Contempt for women

It is obvious that neither dowry customs nor rape can be eliminated by only changing laws; it is vital to change the deeply rooted traditional position of women in society. 'A baby girl is born with the curse of being neglected.' 'Women's bodies are exploited, abused, sold, aged, and burned.' This is what causes their grief and feeds their anger.

It is on record that in India the mortality rate of infant girls is higher than that for infant boys: male babies, 120 and female babies, 131 per 1,000 births. Moreover, women under forty years of age are likely to have shorter life expectations than men. Therefore, the ratio between men and women in the Indian population differs from that in most other countries: 930 women to 1,000 men; and the proportion of women has continued to decrease since the 1960s.

> How did more than twenty million women disappear from our population? The 1971 census shows that there are 20 million fewer women than men in our country. This gap between the numbers has been widening since independence was achieved in 1947. Even though outright female infanticide has been declared illegal, deliberate negligence of girl babies to the point of letting them die is on the increase. Often, when the question is raised of a declining gender proportion within a ratio, people dismiss it as an academic question as if it were a matter of arithmetic and statistics, but this is a life and death issue for women.
> (*Manushi*, No. 7, 1981)

Indian women are deeply concerned about this issue.

Japanese intellectuals, and others like them, who glorify India as a 'country of mysticism', hear none of the cries of the oppressed. Even though India is proud of its spiritually oriented civilization, it is a society that maintains discrimination by a class and caste system. It is also a society that is marked, at times, by merciless violence. In such a society, it is the women who are most seriously damaged, particularly poor women of low or outcaste status. They are denied full lives from the moment of their birth solely because they are born female. Hindu Manu scriptures teach, 'As daughters, women should obey their fathers; as wives, obey their husbands; and, as widows, obey their sons. They should never think of being independent.' Literature and the arts also urge Hindu women to practise such virtues as devotion, sacrifice, fidelity, and obedience.

How similar these teachings are to the Confucian teaching of the 'Three Obediences' so well known in Japan! The issues that preoccupy women's movements in India are, in fact, not so very different from Japanese women's concerns. Unhappily, the ideology of discrimination against women, that takes an extreme form in India, is, in fact, surprisingly universal.

The author with Filipino migrant workers' families (Manila 1984).

Kamadu and her children taking shelter in a Hindu shrine (Rawan, Malaysia 1984).

A six-storey brothel full of prostitutes and customers (Narayanganji, Bangladesh 1982).

Village women making jute bags (a suburb of Dhaka, 1982).

Mother with child picking fallen fruits of oil palm (Rawan, Malaysia 1984).

Cathy, Filipina maid, takes care of her employer's baby (Singapore 1984).

Filipina women workers at newly opened Japanese factory in Bataen export processing zone (Maliveres, Philippines 1985).

Pat Pong bar girls enjoy learning English at a class organized by EMPOWER (Bangkok 1986).

Licensed hostesses waiting for VD check at social hygiene clinic in Olongapo (Philippines 1983).

Young mother mourning at the tomb of her son killed in **Kwangju** uprising (Korea 1985).

Poor housing for women workers – a squatter area
(Maliveres, Philippines 1985).

Ms Fatima.

Sister Christine Tau in the slum where she was living
(Manila 1984).

Pakistani feminists preparing placards for anti-Islamization
demonstration (Lahore 1983).

Huge anti-rape demonstration by Indian women in New Delhi.

A family grieving around the remains of their daughter, a victim of
dowry murder (New Delhi 1981).

Nepalese girls escaped from red light district of Bombay staying at
Women's welfare home (Kathmandu, Nepal 1984).

Nepalese prostitutes waiting for customers outside the brothels
(Bombay 1983).

Young women working at a cheroot factory (Pegu, Burma 1983).

International Women's Day rally organized by Gabriela just after the ousting of Marcos (Manila 1986).

Filipina girls at a disco for US soldiers in Olongapo city (Philippines 1983).

Pakistani women protesting Islamization policies, confronted by armed police (Lahore 1983).

Ms Takasao Doi giving a solidarity speech at the women's rally
organized by Gabriela (Manila 1986).

Ms Hong at children's centre in Maurok Dong slum (Korea 1985).

7.

Religion and Women's Perspectives:
From Oppressive Tools to Liberating Force

Nepalese women

I first visited Nepal in spring 1984. This beautiful, land-locked country, dominated by the Himalayas, lies between two big powers: China to the north and India to the south. A largely feudal society, Nepal opened its doors to the world only in the 1950s. Apart from the southern lowlands, this is a mountainous terrain and its population of sixteen million comprises numerous tribal groups, speaking more than thirty-six different languages. Culturally and economically Indian influence is strong, and twenty percent of the population is Hindu.

Marta Sharma, a midwife in Kathmandu told me that:

> If the newborn baby is a boy, it's a joyous time, and gifts are distributed in a festive mood to the neighbours. However, if a baby girl is born, her mother begins to cry and the atmosphere is gloomy, like a wake. The mother is blamed for this misfortune, and she is badly treated. She is not given food after the pain of her labour.

She has assisted in as many as 1,200 deliveries in the rural areas, and one of her roles is to console and encourage *buhari* (daughter-in-law brides) who grieve when they give birth to female babies. As Marta said:

> What a difference between a boy and a girl, even when it is the same newborn life. From the moment a female is born into this world she is considered to be a curse – the beginning of a woman's life of mistreatment and misery.

On leaving Kathmandu and entering a rural village, I saw a group of women bent under the heavy loads of firewood they carried on their backs; barefoot and walking silently, they wore discoloured saris, tied at the waist with broad sashes, in the style of the Newar people. Meanwhile the men of the village strolled about in long white tunics worn over trousers, with black caps on their heads. I was reminded of my visit to North India when I travelled the Ganges River upstream, deep into a Himalayan mountain village to interview a woman who had started the Chipko Movement. There, too, I saw women bent under the heavy burdens on their backs while the men drank tea and played cards at the teahouse. It was quite shocking to see this rigid sexual division of labour that seemingly imposes hard work only on the women.

> Some women commit suicide because of their deep despair. This year, in the district where I [Marta Sharma] am working, two mothers and one young girl hanged themselves; another woman jumped into the river with her baby daughter in her arms: the baby drowned but the mother was saved.

Marta also told me that:

> Young village girls are deceived by agents and sold to brothels in red-light districts in and around Bombay. They are so poor and oppressed in village life that they are anxious to get out into the world. Illiterate, they have no idea what will happen to them in a foreign country.

They leave one hell for another. The Ministry of Welfare of the Nepalese government estimates that as many as 50,000 Nepalese women, known as cage girls, are in brothels. In the suburbs of Kathmandu I visited a Women's Welfare Home for girls who escape from brothels to save their lives. Uniformly dressed in blue saris, nine girls were learning reading and writing, dressmaking, and knitting. Around fourteen to fifteen years old, they had been confined in cages and beaten by the 'madam'. Fed inadequate meals, they serviced five to six customers a day; many of them suffer from tuberculosis and venereal disease. In this home, after having passed through such an ordeal, they are making preparations to start a new life. Most of them do not want to return to their home villages because, as Marta Sharma said, as women, there is little hope for them in village life.

Life in a mountain village
My visit to Nepal was too brief for me to visit remote mountain villages

as this would have meant journeying by bus or walking for many days. But this is how Rochan Karlci, a thirty-one-year-old former student activist, described to me the situation of mountain village women:

I have just come back from Jumla in the north-western mountain area. I was shocked to see poverty such as I had never imagined it. It is very cold there and, in small, mud huts without windows, the villagers were burning wood for heating and cooking. The women's faces were blackened with soot, except for around their eyes where they wipe away the tears from the smoke, or around their mouths when they eat. Their food usually consists of a piece of potato and apple, because it is an apple-producing area. Since they have so little water, they do not bathe neither do they cut their hair. Their clothes are so dirty the smell is terrible!

Even in the Lalitpur district near Kathmandu, women are still confined in the home. Some have never seen a bus, or used soap, or tasted sugar. For half the year they have no crops so they have to survive on a thin rice gruel. Since the women's portion is whatever is left over, they are especially gaunt. At age seven or eight, young girls are already fetching water and firewood, tending the cattle, and caring for younger brothers and sisters. Some of them are sent to work as servants in other homes. Our maid came to us when she was only seven years old. Usually, girls marry at twelve or thirteen. They are forced to work hard as *buhari*, and give birth almost every year; some of their babies die. When only in their thirties, these women are already old.

Another woman to whom I talked was Rajya Shree Pokharel, a forty-five-year-old teacher of home economics at Padmar Kanya College, the only college for women in Nepal. Each year as an exercise in social work, she takes students to stay in a village for a week. They live with the village women and teach them nutrition, personal hygiene, use of sanitary latrines and how to cultivate vegetables. She said:

Women are not treated as human beings. They have to get up at three o'clock in the morning and do all the housework; in the afternoon, they must work on the farm. They work the whole day but their husbands listen to the radio, smoke cigarettes, order their wives around, and quickly eat up the food the women have cooked. Wives eat only the leftovers. Even if they don't feel well, they cannot say so, nor can they take a rest. If they die, their husbands will get another wife after the required wait of forty-five days. But if a woman's husband dies she is not allowed to remarry, but must remain a widow for the rest of her life. Husbands are masters, wives are slaves. Even today, wives wash their husbands' feet every morning and, in some districts, must even worship their husbands. In urban areas, the younger generation is changing, but much too slowly.

The average daily working hours for men are seven, but for women, eleven. In terms of average lifespans, the Nepalese woman lives only 44.5 years, three years fewer than a Nepalese man; this is one of the few countries where the men tend to outlive the women. Even if a female baby is not killed, and she survives beyond infancy, she is not sent to school and is forced to marry at an early age. As a daughter-in-law, she will suffer from malnutrition and cruelly hard work; her life will be very short.

In his memoirs, Dr Kawahara, Director of the Asian Health Institute, Nagoya, Japan, who was at one time a surgeon in Nepal, describes how one day, a pale-faced peasant woman came into a hospital from a very remote village. She had a bleeding skin cancer on her leg. The doctor told her that unless her leg was amputated, her life could not be saved. But this mother of four children, the eldest only six, would not consent to the operation. 'If I die,' she said, 'my husband will remarry and his new wife will take care of my children. But, if I lose my leg, I cannot do the housework such as fetching water, and my whole family will suffer.' Thus, she preferred death to life without walking.

Hinduism's concept of women

Why do women have to be treated so badly? Of course, because of the economic factor, poverty is endemic, but why, in poor families, is it the women who suffer more than the men? Here the impact of Hinduism cannot be disregarded.

Between 1500 and 500 BC, Hinduism spread throughout India and surrounding areas, and the caste system was institutionalized. As we noted in the previous chapter, the Hindu Manu scriptures teach life-long obedience for women to their fathers, husbands or sons; their teaching resembles the three obediences of Confucianism. Manu Scripture also teaches, 'drums, idiots, untouchables, cattle, and women should always be beaten to make them work'.

In those days, women were considered unclean because they menstruate. When in 1982 I was in Bali Island, in Indonesia, I visited a Hindu temple where, to my surprise, there was a large notice at the entrance saying, 'Menstruating women are not clean; therefore, they are not allowed to enter the precincts of the temple.' The 2,000-year-old concept of women is still alive today.

To be born a woman is considered to be retribution for bad behaviour in a previous life. 'O, why am I born a woman? I know already. An unhappy fate awaits me,' wrote a Nepalese woman poet. Full of grief, it is a woman's poem that she felt compelled to write as she knows she is 'destined for the role of disciplined daughter, submissive wife, self-sacrificing mother, and dominating mother-in-law, and especially to fulfil the painful role of daughter-in-law.'

I visited the home of Menaka Rajbhandari, a young woman activist who lived near the Pashupati Hindu Temple in Kathmandu. We enjoyed a reunion two years after we had met at the Thailand conference Asian Cultural Forum on Development (ACFOD). The whole area was enveloped in smoke from the cremation of human bodies on the nearby riverbank. We were taking a walk in the temple grounds when Menaka told me:

> Hindu religion reinforces the inbred discrimination and inequality between men and women. The sacred concept of Dharma enjoins everyone to perform the divinely appointed role only. No one is supposed to step beyond the bounds of caste or gender. Women are forced to remain inferior. It imposes on women a 'culture of silence', and women accept their fate without protest.

Menaka, still in her twenties, speaking with a gentle smile, is not very tall, is very active, a dynamic person bouncing around like a rubber ball. After visiting a rural village in her student days, she became involved in women's issues. Having worked for a time as a primary school teacher she has now started a literacy class for village women in Sindhupalchok, a remote mountain area.

Speaking enthusiastically, Menaka said, 'I am helping them learn to read and write for their own consciousness-raising; that is, for them as women to understand their situation and to stand up to change it.' She had just married her university classmate and she continued, 'If I have a baby girl, I will never grieve because of it. I shall treat her just the same as a male child, and bring her up to be an independent woman.' She herself was trying to practise a new lifestyle and break away from

Hindu tradition. Her courage and determination were really moving, for when I first visited her country, I was conscious of the heavy burden of the old traditions she was proposing to defy.

Mata Sharma and Rochan Karlci, actively involved in health and welfare programmes for the liberation of women from poverty and discrimination, and Rajya Shree Pokharel and Menaka, married to partners of their own choosing and devoting themselves to educational activities for women, are themselves members of the economically better-off intellectual class, but they are also a minority who resist Hindu tradition and live with the firm belief that 'women are also human beings'. My encounter with these pioneer women who were trying to open up a new future for Nepal gave me a strong feeling of hope for this country.

Women in an Islamic world

In Islamic countries, where the edicts against women are even more strict than those of Hinduism, women who used to be confined by *chador* (a veil that covers the face and body) and *chardiwari* (the custom of confining women to within four walls) are beginning to speak out. I saw the dynamics of a power relation that emerges when the stronger the oppression of Islamic tradition, the greater is the will to fight back.

Entering the Islamic world from largely Hindu or Buddhist countries it is surprising to see so few women; as I noticed when I visited Bangladesh and Pakistan. I was astounded to see that most people on the streets, even in the big cities of Lahore and Karachi, were men.

The present government [Pakistan], that took power by military coup d'état in 1977, has been forcefully imposing Islamization and an anti-women policy – a return to Islamic tradition. We are now under the worst oppression since independence in 1947; we call it the 'new dark age'. Since the Khomeini revolution in Iran in 1979, Islamic fundamentalism has spread all over the Islamic world. Encouraged by this situation, and supported by fanatic and stubborn fundamentalists, our military regime began to introduce discriminatory laws against women. These men in power are afraid of women; probably that is why they want to suppress them. We can no longer stand it, and that's why we will fight back now. We are waging *jihad* [holy war] of women.

This I was told by Shamim Anwar, history teacher at the prestigious

Kinnaird College for Women in Lahore.

According to women in Lahore, unbelievable things have been done against women in the name of Islam. Immediately after the coup d'état, President Zia-ul-Haq had spoken on television and ordered women to abide by the rules of *chador* and *chardiwari*. Dr Ahmad, Director of the Koran Research Institute in Lahore, also appeared on TV and said, 'Working women should put on *chador*, and men should carry canes when they go out so that they can beat women who are not wearing the veil.' Pakistani women were forbidden to compete in the Asian Games or in the World Cup hockey matches in Kuala Lumpur.

The segregation of women from men is the core of Islamic tradition; women are confined to the home, and must cover themselves completely when they go out. In many Arab countries, before the advent of Islam, people lived a nomadic life. Women had sexual freedom, often under a matriarchy; they could choose and accept men as husbands in their own tents; the women also retained custody of the children. The advent of Islam was between the sixth and seventh centuries, which was also a transitional period to patriarchy, and a time of flourishing trade when the Arab people began to settle in more permanent communities.

The concept of women on the part of Islam's founder, the Prophet Mohammed, contained many contradictions. During his sixty-two years of life, he married an older woman with whom he lived for twenty-five years. It is said that in the twelve years after her death, he married as many as twelve women, one after another.

The sacred book of Islam, the Koran, teaches that men and women are equal and have equal rights; men and women can develop equally, morally and spiritually. Women may, therefore, participate in educational training and religious activities such as prayer in the mosque. On the other hand, it is written in the Koran that women were created in order to provide physical, mental and spiritual comfort to men; the discriminatory concept of marriage derives from this. Marriage is considered to be obligatory and any woman (or man) who is eligible for marriage but remains unmarried is despised. Fathers who have daughters still unmarried may not make pilgrimages to Mecca. Polygamy is accepted and men have four wives; women, however have no freedom to choose their marriage partners. Divorce is severely frowned upon but husbands may demand one at any time. Wives are thus placed in the weaker position and must bear any abuse. Today illiterate women are taught by the mullahs (Islamic teachers) to believe that wearing the veil is more important than participating in religious activities; and the veil is a psychological as well as a physical restriction. Women are thus forced into total dependence on the men in their family.

Sharmim Anwar, looking back on fourteen centuries of Islamic history, said:

> The Koran advocates the ideology of men and women as being equals but reflects the historical and social conditions of those early days by imposing polygamy and purdah [the practice of hiding women from the view of men and strangers]. Later men interpreted the Koran from a sexist point of view, and this discriminatory interpretation became well-established. As a result, women are neither allowed nor expected to be independent, and are kept in subjugation.

The Pakistani military regime wanted a return to such Islamic tradition by establishing or amending a series of Islamic laws that would further debase the status of women. There were four legal issues involved. The first was the Hadood Ordinance (1979), which not only revived medieval punishments such as whipping and stoning, but also abolished the distinction between rape and adultery. Consequently, rapists were not punished because, as in adultery, four male witnesses are required to prove guilt. The second was the Islamic Law of Evidence (1984) that requires two female witnesses where one male witness would suffice in cases of oral evidence; women are, therefore, treated as half persons. In this same vein, the third legal issue was the Blood Money Law, which decrees that in a case of murder, compensation to the family of a female victim is only half that paid to the family of a male victim; the punishment for a female found guilty of murder is, however, the same as for a male.

The fourth legal issue was the Family Law Ordinance. The government considered the present Ordinance, amended in 1961 as a result of women's struggle, to be non-Islamic and wanted it repealed. The main points of contention are: a ban on child marriages with a minimum age of eighteen for men and sixteen for women; requirement of marriage registration; limitations on polygamy (first wife's consent and good reason required); and correction to inequality in case of divorce (a wife may also be allowed to demand divorce).

In 1981, to counter such an Islamization policy, women in Pakistan formed a Women's Action Forum (WAF). They struggled courageously, fearing neither arrest nor imprisonment. They organized demonstrations, which were banned under martial law at that time, and were condemned and accused of being 'non-Islamic'. They never gave up however, and forcefully expressed themselves in various groups.

International Workshop of Women from Muslim Countries

But what is Islam? Is Islam a vision or is it merely a ritualistic exercise? If it is the former, then we can be judged *only* by God. If it is the latter, then perhaps men *can* judge us. The spirit of Islam comes from God. It addresses itself to all believing men *and* women. But the ritual, or the interpretation of God's message comes from men. [Muslim] Women have always been discouraged from religious interpretation. This is no accident; women have always been excluded from religious discourse. This exclusion is a matter of deliberate policy to keep women out of the circuits of power, and to deprive them of the right to control their own lives. Even when religion is used as liberation ideology, women and the feminist dimension are not addressed. And indeed, where Islam has successfully brought a form of liberation, history proves that women have been further suppressed. A classic example of this is the recent transformation in Iran. This order of things *must* be changed. Muslim women all over the world are aware of this. Slowly but *surely* they are getting together to challenge the situation and to retrieve for themselves the essence of the liberation message, the essence of themselves, and the essence of justice.

This powerful speech was delivered by Nighat Said Khan, a member of Simorgh, Women's Resource and Publication Centre in Lahore, at the International Workshop of Women from Muslim Countries in Lahore, Pakistan in 1986 which was attended by women from Muslim countries, and countries with large Muslim minorities, from Algiers in Africa to Malaysia in South-east Asia. They spent four days in heated discussion on oppression and liberation of Muslim women. They concluded that:

Islam and Islamic culture are a complex reality. This complexity is distorted by the West in terms of the way the West views Islam. But the West also has a contradictory position on Islam. On the one hand, it operates an active anti-Islamic campaign, and on the other, it supports fundamentalism. In both cases, however, it does this for its own political purposes.

A further conclusion was that the manifestation of Islam differs from one social reality to another. For example, the custom of dowry and wearing the veil are personal statutes that change from country to country. This reality demystifies the universal aspect of Islam in practice, for Islam is defined by its historical and sociological context, not by a common framework.

> At the same time, Muslim countries, capitalist or socialist, have in common the fact that there is no Muslim state that is not dictatorial and oppressive, especially as far as women are concerned. This oppression of women rests on imperialism and capitalism, and on fundamentalism, which is connected to and encouraged by the first two, as also is patriarchy.

Finally, the participants declared:

> As feminists who live in the Muslim world, we are searching and struggling for a new non-patriarchal and just society. Feminists in Muslim countries must join hands and from within we must change our Muslim world.

The Hidden Face of Eve

The woman who symbolized Muslim women's struggle for liberation at the July 1985 Nairobi Conference closing the United Nations Women's Decade was Nawal El Saadawi, an Egyptian with beautiful grey hair. She is a doctor, who had once held the post of Director of Public Health in the Egyptian government, but had been dismissed because, as a feminist pioneer, she had written a number of books advocating the liberation of Arab women. Among the twenty-two books she has authored, *The Hidden Face of Eve – Women in the Arab World* (1980), is an especially moving story that begins with an account of the pain of circumcision forced upon her by custom at the age of six. Now, she is calling on Islam as a weapon of resistance rather than as a tool for oppressing women as it is used by the ruling class.

> We are working hard, especially in the area of women's education. For example, we are raising political consciousness with the slogan, 'Take off the veil covering your brain!' Even if you remove your veil, if your consciousness remains covered you have no power. Women's issues such as equality with men are really political issues. Neither peace nor development is possible without justice. We are combining the class struggle against bad economic development, such as new colonialism, with the struggle against patriarchy that discriminates against women.

'Beyond the Veil'

Another charismatic Muslim woman is Fatima Mernissi, a forty-five-year-old Moroccan sociologist, a participant in the 1984 International Conference on Third World Development Crisis in Penang, Malaysia. She is internationally well known as the author of *Beyond the Veil, Male–Female Dynamics in Muslim Society* (1975). Tall and visually striking, wearing a loose, flowing dress, bared to the shoulders, when she spoke her audience was spellbound. She was attacked with sexist comments by an Indian man of Gandhian philosophy and a male chauvinist interpretation of history, and by a Pakistani man, both of whom were thoroughly and competently neutralized by her profound knowledge and sharp satire. The conference participants were silent with amazement! It seemed to me that she must be displaying the endurance and strength required of women who live in a harsh desert climate.

During one conference session, Fatima Mernissi talked quite frankly with the director of the women's section of the Muslim party in Malaysia, who was completely concealed by a black veil: 'You should interpret the Koran and other scriptures with your own brain; it seems that what you've been saying is influenced by men's thinking.' One by one, Fatima rebutted each fundamentalist Islamic idea of the Malaysian woman with her own interpretation. Her confidence and spirit made me feel that women were taking back Islam, monopolized by men for many centuries.

What Fatima Mernissi wanted to show in *Beyond the Veil* was that Islam segregates women because men are afraid of women's strong sexual power. In the Western world of Christianity, women are considered passive (powerless) and sexuality is viewed negatively, while in the Islamic world, sexuality is perceived as a positive factor. In her book she concludes that to change the relationship of men and women in the Muslim world means 'revolutionary restructuring of the total society'. She says:

> What the Arab world faces is not whether to change or not but how fast to change. Feminism and economic development should be combined because both the men and the women in the Third World are suffering from exploitation and want. Arab leaders have the obligation to realize economic growth and to plan for a future without exploitation and want. For this purpose, all human and material resources should be utilized, and women are a very important factor in achieving such a future.

Fatima sharply criticized Western colonial rule and the new colonialism, and emphasized the 'hidden power' of Muslim women above that of Western women because she considers that women should play a central role in creating a new future in the Arab world. She herself in her powerful speech and manner, is living proof of all that she proposed and this convinced me that the liberation of Islamic women is making steady progress.

The Buddhist world and women

In many Asian countries, except Japan, religion is an indispensable part of life. In addition to Hindu and Islamic countries there are a number of Buddhist countries: Sri Lanka, Thailand, Burma, Laos, and Kampuchea; countries in which there is still strong belief in Theravada Buddhism. (Theravada or Hinayana Buddhism is the first of two strands of Buddhism, and emphasizes personal salvation through one's own efforts. The later strand – Mahayana – emphasizes salvation by faith only.) In these Buddhist countries, women are much less oppressed and the tradition of matriarchy has not been totally destroyed. Women are more independent and free, and lead active lives.

Buddhism originated in the sixth century BC as a sort of criticism against the caste system of Hinduism.

> Buddhism is the first religion in the world to establish a community of ordained women on the basis that women can achieve equal salvation with men. According to the Hindu Manu scripture, women are possessions to be handed down under the protection of men. Women were not allowed to perform rituals on their own. Within this social context, Buddhism opened up new horizons, and Buddhist women stepped out of their expected roles to fulfil their ideal roles, not only as wives and mothers, but now as propagators of this new religion in the same capacity as their male counterparts.

Thus Chatsumarn Kabilsingh of the liberal arts faculty at Thammasat University in Bangkok explained to me. She went on to say that in the beginning, Buddhist nuns were treated as the equals of monks, but after the Buddha died, and under the influence of Hindu culture, they became more like servants to the monks. They spent so much time taking care of the monks that they had no time to attend to their own spiritual practices. Finally, the order of nuns died out in Theravada Buddhist countries.

In Bangkok, a city filled with beautiful *wat* (Buddhist temples) with golden domes, I frequently saw nuns in faded pink or shabby white robes sitting at the temple gates, begging for alms from the passers-by. In contrast to orange-robed monks, the nuns somehow looked wretched. A Thai feminist group, Friends of Women, is rightly critical of the fact that the nuns are treated like beggars. This group also accuses Buddhism of being responsible for the expansion of prostitution in Thailand. In northern Thailand, in a very poor area from which young girls are being sold, there is a luxurious monastery, largely built with donations from these young women who earn money by selling their bodies. The Friends of Women also asserts that some temples are involved in the flesh trade of young girls.

Sukanya Hantrakul, a Thai journalist dealing with prostitution issues, was critical of the Buddhist concept of women in a presentation to an Asian workshop in Melbourne, Australia, in 1983:

> One basic idea in Buddhism is *karma*. This means that the sum of actions in one's previous lives determines an individual's present status. To be born a woman in this life means there was an inadequate store of merit in her previous lives. Thus women are put into socially and economically disadvantaged positions. Also, the double standard that only men are allowed sexual freedom is the cultural background that promotes rampant prostitution in Thailand.

She emphasized that in order to understand the reality of this double standard one must know that (as we saw in Chapter 5) there are more than 700,000 prostitutes compared with only 300,000 monks; this is not simply a statistical analysis but should be seen in the light of Buddhist cultural tradition.

Confucian concept of women

The East Asian countries of China, Korea, Japan, and Vietnam are countries of Mahayana Buddhism and, at the same time, deeply influenced by Confucian cultural mores. Confucianism is not a religion but a system of ethics that oppresses women, as is demonstrated in its infamous 'three obediences' to father as child, to husband as wife, and to son as widow.

In China, before the 1949 Revolution, the terrible plight of women was almost inexpressible. As Mao Ze-dong pointed out, women had to endure the oppression of four powers: politics, religion, relatives, and husband. And the Confucian idea of respecting man and despising woman has not been overcome even yet. The Chinese still want to have sons and the 'one-child policy' now in effect is a very serious social problem.

The major task of the feminist movement in Korea, Taiwan, and Hong Kong is also consciousness-raising to overcome hundreds of years of Confucian ideology. Japanese women are also bound by traditional gender roles as the dominant social concept in combination with Confucian ideology. Clearly, to break through this barrier is a massive task.

Christianity

Finally, Christianity has taken root in some of the countries of Asia where it is a minority religion. The one exception to this is the Roman Catholic country of the Philippines where liberation theology is practised. And in South Korea where there are at least seven million Christians exerting some social influence, Minjung (people) theology is widespread. This theology is critical of a Christianity connected with the ruling powers or colonial rule, and a Christian theology of oppressed people is growing.

Believing in this new perspective, more and more Catholic nuns and Protestant women are joining in activities to protect women's human rights in villages, urban slums, and factories throughout Asia. The Christian Conference of Asia is a network of churches in Asian countries, and its Secretary for Women's Concerns is engaged in addressing women's problems in Asian countries.

The Asian Women's Theological Network was formed in 1982, and seeks to create a new theology based on the realities of the Third World from a woman's point of view. Revd Sunai Park, a Korean woman pastor living in Singapore, is the co-ordinator of this network that publishes a newsletter, *In God's Image*. In order to link Christianity and Asian feminism, they are attempting to have a dialogue with other religions from a woman's perspective. This new movement has begun to effect change in the Western European and male-dominated Christian theology toward theological perspectives of Third World women.

Asian women are radically questioning religions that direct them to accept the suffering of this world as destiny and force them to endure. Religion is changing from a tool for oppressing women to a weapon for their liberation.

8.
A Tradition of Matriarchy:
The Vitality of Burmese Women

Introduction

To many Japanese, Burma is an unknown country. During World War Two, Burma was invaded by 300,000 Japanese troops of whom 180,000 were killed. Thus, for this generation, Burma is always associated with war, and the post-war generation's image is derived from a well-known novel by Michio Takeyama, *Burmese Harp*; the younger people have no image at all. This is not surprising as Burma has operated a closed-country policy since the 1962 coup d'état, and the resulting military dictatorship established a Burmese-style socialism. In the 1980s, however, the country did open up, even to foreign tourists, but only on one-week visas; the number of visitors is quite small, about 40,000 each year.

In 1983 I had an opportunity to spend two weeks in this unknown country. To my surprise, Bangkok and Burma's capital city, Rangoon, are separated by less than one hour by air, but despite this proximity, I found myself in a completely different world when I arrived in Rangoon. I visited the ancient capital Mandalay, Pagan with its historical ruins, and Pegu with its famous reclining Buddha, as well as some other cities, and was fascinated by all I saw.

What did I find that was so attractive? First, the warmth, gentleness and kindness of the Burmese people. They have a deep Buddhist faith and enjoy a rich spiritual life. Economic growth has been very slow; the goal is an 'exploitation-free society', and, unlike the trend in some other Asian countries, Burma's economic structure is not based on a search for profit in sexual exploitation, or the use of child labour. Burma does not accept foreign investment by private companies, so I did not see foreigners enjoying special privileges, as in many other countries where transnational corporations are operating. Internationally, Burma operates a policy of strict non-aligned neutrality, which has kept it free from international conflicts.

For both men and women, high-ranking officials and common people alike, in Rangoon and in the rural areas, the popular choice of dress is the national costume, the *longyi* (long wrap-around skirt). Not only because of their conservatism and for economic reasons, but also, it seemed to me, as an expression of national pride or strong nationalism.

Of course, there are many problems. The military regime holds power and there is no democracy. There are still insurgent groups among minority tribal people; and there are serious economic difficulties, such as a high rate of unemployment of educated people because of priority in agricultural development rather than industrialization. The black market expands to supplement the shortages of daily necessities.

High status of women

One of the little-known aspects of Burmese culture, and a new discovery for me is the impressively high status of women. The Burmese women whom I met during my two-week stay were vivacious and attractive.

Even before I left Singapore I was impressed by the warmth and strength of Burmese women through my acquaintance with Dr Ma Win Kyi. She is an expert on Hansen's Disease (leprosy), and was staying with her brother in Singapore. Always she wore the beautiful *longyi*, and could be seen walking with light steps along the skyscraper-lined streets of Singapore. When I told her that I would be visiting Burma, she promptly contacted her close friends in Rangoon, asking them to take care of me. She gave me lots of instructions on whom I should meet, where I must visit, what kinds of events I could not miss, and so on. I had never before received such kind and detailed orientation for my journeys to other countries.

On my arrival in Rangoon, I discovered that there are a number of women doctors there, in fact about half of all doctors in Burma are women. I met a neurosurgeon, who had studied in Japan and his wife, a paediatrician working in a children's hospital. This hospital has 500 beds, and eighty percent of the doctors are women. In the central maternity hospital, there are only two men among the forty doctors there. This is certainly a contrast to Japan where most doctors are men. Dr Ma Win Kyi is only one of many women doctors who are experts on Hansen's Disease.

In Burma, the most elite profession is considered to be that of medical doctor; and of all the institutes of higher education, entry to the Rangoon Medical College is the most difficult to attain. Many women pass the entrance examination in competition with men. In Burmese society women are not considered to be inferior to men and both men and women receive the same education. This is very different from most other Asian countries; for example, Bangladesh, Burma's close neighbour, is well known for its high illiteracy rate, which is more than eighty percent for Bangladeshi women. As Gunnar Myrdal observed, in *Asian Drama*; 'In Burma, different from other South Asian and southeast Asian countries, the education system is not disadvantageous to women.' He attributes the reason for this to Buddhism, which is more egalitarian than other Asian religions. Traditionally, education at the temple was widely practised, and the literacy rate is about seventy percent.

Women are also active in the education field. Daw Tin Tin, a close friend of Ma Win Kyi, and who took me to see the reclining Buddha in the old city of Pegu, is the Principal of Burma's largest school for women with 6,000 students. Mother of two sons and two daughters, she is a veteran educationalist with a long career. At twenty-two years of age she became a teacher and taught in the classroom for thirty-two years before becoming Principal sixteen years ago. 'Our school has a primary, junior high, and senior high school, and the majority of teachers are women – ninety percent in the primary school, eighty percent in the junior high, and seventy percent in the senior high,' she told me.

In the evening I attended a dinner party in one of the dormitories, the residence of 300 students from rural districts, many of whom were members of minority tribes. After dinner, they performed wonderful dances and songs drawn from the various tribal traditions. Principal Daw Tin Tin said, 'We try to educate them to be independent women. This evening's performance was planned entirely by the students themselves, who, until last week, were studying hard for exams, and they did quite well.' She was clearly proud of her students.

The level of scholarship at this women's school is never lower than that of any men's school, and many students gain entry to university. They study very hard but they also enjoy themselves. I was fascinated by the beauty of the students dressed in their own traditional costumes. As Daw Tin Tin passed by, they greeted her so elegantly: with their fingers touched lightly to their lips, they whispered, 'Goodnight, Madam'. These students are educated to become independent and charming Burmese women, and most of them will pursue professional careers after graduation.

Urban women

Thirty-five-year-old Mya My Tui teaches in a suburban primary school. The eldest daughter of a family whose business is making robes for Buddhist monks and nuns, she chose to be independent rather than work in the family business. She took the examination for Rangoon University several times until she finally won a place in the mathematics department. 'I had about 100 classmates at the university, sixty men and forty women, and twenty-five of the women are now working; many are teachers,' she said. In her present school, with an enrolment of more than 300 students, there are six teachers, all of whom are women.

Mya My Tui, who was unmarried at the time of our conversation, told me, 'In Burma, there is no social pressure to marry. I don't want to get married unless I meet a nice partner.'

The Rangoon School for the Deaf was established by a woman and also has a woman principal, Daw Mya Yi. After graduating from university, she became a teacher but resigned during World War II to be married. After the war, she returned to teaching and has been in charge of this school since 1962. She devotes herself to the education of about 200 deaf children from three to sixteen years of age. In this school, there are twenty teachers only one of whom is a man and he provides vocational training in woodwork. In the infant class I saw a young woman giving training in pronunciation, illustrating her lesson by using stuffed animals; in another class, a middle-aged women was directing mentally retarded children in drawing. Both of these teachers treated their pupils with care and tenderness, which compensated for the somewhat sparse facilities and equipment.

Many of Burma's enterprises are state-run, and the employees are government officials. There are many women section chiefs, and among department heads and deputy heads, women are not unusual. May Kim Chaw, (Ma Win Kyi's closest friend and a wonderful guide during my visit) had just resigned her position as a government ministry department head, and was hoping to become a director of broadcasting. This graduate of Rangoon University and mother of two said, 'I have never thought of being just a housewife. Most of my university classmates are working somewhere or in business of some kind.' There are many couples where the husband is a government official and the wife is in business. One reason is because government salaries are quite low, only 300 kyat (9,000 yen) and a wife can earn several times that amount in business.

Women's active participation in society is not limited to the highly educated, intellectual women; grass-roots women are also hard at work. In Rangoon and other cities, I saw many women, cheeks powdered with *tanaka* (Burmese powder), engaged in lively trading in the markets. At around two o'clock in the afternoon at Rangoon's central station, a train arrives and unloads women carrying big bundles on to already crowded platforms. They are carrying smuggled goods from across the Thai border where they trade textiles for daily necessities, medicines, food, and so forth, and will then sell these items at the nearby black market. It is said that this black economy accounts for more than half the entire Burmese economy; the women who engage in this business include university graduates as well as the less highly educated.

Burma is not yet industrialized and most of its factories are very small workshops. In the old town of Pegu, famous for its *cheroots* (small Burmese 'cigars'), I visited one of these factories. On the second floor of a bungalow, about 20 women, all wearing the traditional *longyi*, were seated on the floor, working. Near the window, rows of women sat facing each other, and each one was busily wrapping shredded *shan* leaves (a Burmese plant) in corn husks. I was amazed at how fast they worked. One of them, a twenty-two-year-old veteran of nine years, could wrap as many as 700 pieces a day. In another corner of the room, one woman was making bundles of 100 pieces each without even counting. She was so skilful with her hands that bundles of *cheroots* seemed to pile up instantly in front of her.

A tall, middle-aged woman, the manager of this factory, said, 'We produce 30,000 packages [100 pieces in each package] every month. Most of the employees are young single women. Housewives also do this work at home. If they work hard they can earn at least 200 kyat (6,000 yen) a month.' This factory had a family atmosphere about it; the *cheroot* is produced as a cottage industry far removed from a modern factory.

Cheroot production is traditionally women's work because of their nimble fingers. In markets and on farms I saw old women relaxing, smoking *cheroots*. It is a cheap habit that does not lead to tobacco smoking, neither does it have harmful properties as does tobacco, and the people continue to enjoy it.

In the ancient capital Mandalay, and in Pagan, there are a number of traditional craft workshops in silversmithing, ivory processing, lacquer-ware, silk weaving, and marble sculpturing. There I saw not only male artisans but also women who applied themselves to this highly skilled work. In a marble sculpture workshop, young girls with chisels were carving a huge nose on a statue of Buddha. In another shop, young women weavers were using gold- and silver-coloured thread to produce beautiful textiles for the *longyi*. Each time I saw Burmese men and women working together in equal positions, I was reminded of how greatly this differed from so many other Asian countries.

Rural women

In many countries, only the men work on the farms while the women take care of the arts and crafts, as well as the home and children. This division of labour was once also common in China and still prevails in many Asian countries. In Bangladesh, I was very much surprised to see that the typists, receptionists, and tea-service jobs in the city offices are all filled by men. And, in the rural areas, I did not see many women working on the farms. By contrast, in the rural villages in Burma, women are actively engaged in agricultural labour. Since Burma is an agricultural country, women play a very important role in the economy.

Outside Rangoon, you will see nothing but vast areas of paddy fields. I visited a farmhouse that was built high up off the ground and, as it was just after the rice harvest, rice straw was piled up around the house. Underneath the elevated house floor, cows were lying down. A sunburned farmer told me, 'We have just finished sending rice to the government and now we can relax.' Farmland is owned by the state, and each family is assigned a sixteen-acre field. Even if one additional helper is available, it does not provide a farmer with enough labour, which is why this farmer's wife, Shi La, has to work so hard.

There are seven children, aged two to eighteen, in this family, and Shi La is pregnant with the eighth child. She must work in the rice paddies until the last minute before delivery. 'We have to make our two daughters help and cannot send them to school,' she said. She also has to take care of four cows, two water buffalo, and some chickens; she is constantly working. 'I already have too many children so I didn't want to have another, but now I am pregnant again. I stopped taking the pill, which gave me a headache all the time. The government wants to increase the population and recommends that we have many children. But this is not easy for women,' Shi La protested.

In most countries in Asia, the government is making efforts to control population growth, but the Burmese government policy is to increase the present thirty-four million to forty million people, in a land that is 1.8 times the size of Japan. Even the words 'family planning' are taboo; 'family counselling' is used instead. Contraceptive pills are smuggled in from Bangladesh or Thailand, and marketed here in Burma. Only recently has the policy been relaxed to allow families with four children to use family-planning techniques. Not only farmers, but even busy career women have four or five children and continue to work. This is an awesome testimony to Burmese women's vitality.

Egalitarian thinking unique to Burma

'Burmese women are reliable and diligent.' Japanese men who were living in Rangoon were unanimous in their praise of Burmese women. They may recognize the contrast to Japanese women. 'Why are Burmese women so strong?' was a question that I asked both Burmese and Japanese at every opportunity.

It is widely believed that, before Buddhism, a matriarchal tradition existed and since Burma has not been overcome by Hinduism, Islam, or Confucianism, this can still be found. During the age of Burmese dynasties from the thirteenth century, women participated in most sections of society: both national and local government, the judiciary, medicine, and arts and literature. There have been queens who ruled with strength and power, and eminent women authors in great numbers. As Lillian Kha Nau told me:

> Burma is located between India and China. Nevertheless, we did not introduce the Indian caste system nor the Chinese system of foot binding. Burmese women have never been covered by the veil. In the early history, our women enjoyed social, political, and religious freedom. They were even more liberated than the women in the Western countries, and they already enjoy the rights that European women are now so vehemently demanding.

She is a biologist who was the International School Principal in Rangoon for sixteen years, and is now an active leader in the YWCA, devoted to leadership training for women. I learned a lot from discussions with her.

Burmese women do not change their names after marriage. The same holds true in Korea but for different reasons. In Korea's historical background, women were so despised that they were accepted as brides but not allowed to use the family names of their husbands, due to the strong influence of Confucianism. In Burma, however, there is no family name, and each person has an individual registration using only his or her personal name. In this sense, a strong appreciation of the equality of men and women permeates the society.

As far as marriage and family are concerned, Burma has neither a dowry system nor a preference for male children such as may be found, for example, in India and other Hindu societies. (For a full discussion of the dowry system and its impact on women, see Chapter 6.) For a short time following a marriage in Burma, it is common for the newly-weds to live with the bride's family until the young couple can achieve economic independence. According to the Burmese way of thinking, the daughter in a family is not given into the groom's family, but the groom is received into the bride's family, and it is the daughter who assumes the responsibility of caring for the aged parents.

Burma also differs from other Asian countries, in that divorce is more easily obtained and property is owned by both men and women. The property that is owned by the woman at the time of her marriage remains in her possession, and the property gained during the marriage is shared equally by husband and wife. Mutually owned property may not be disposed of without both spouses' consent.

In the matter of inheritance, if the husband dies, the wife automatically inherits the property and becomes the family head, responsible for all family matters. And, when the wife also dies, the property is divided equally between her sons and daughters. The daughter who has cared for the deceased mother usually inherits the family home and her mother's jewellery. This matrilineal/matrilocal custom is quite the opposite of the pre-war *ie* (family) system in Japan, elements of which still exist today.

At the 1977 Tehran Conference of Experts held by the Women and Development Asia Pacific Center in Bangkok, Kinshida Lwin from Burma submitted a report, 'Gender Role in Burmese Society'. Describing in detail the legal status of Burmese women, she pointed out:

> The Burmese word for 'parent' means 'mother and father'. The 'mother' comes first, and the children are taught to give love and gratitude to the mother first. . . . Burmese women have pride and confidence. They never think of themselves as inferior to men. Such a positive image of the Burmese woman is described in literature, music, drama, and film.

How very different from Japan!

The barrier of Buddhist ideology

'In reality, men and women are a long way from total equality', was the critical viewpoint of Kha Nau. 'The number of working women is increasing enormously but we have a shortage of child care centres, and husbands do not usually co-operate in doing housework.' The government has no special policy for women, claiming that, 'The equality of men and women has been achieved both socio-economically and legally. Women are not a separate class in Burmese society.'

According to Kha Nau, the reason women's status is not yet truly equal to men's is rooted in Buddhist views on women. Since only men can receive enlightenment, women pray that they will be reborn as men in another life. In this world, only men can become monks; women are forbidden to enter inside the pagodas. The junior high school daughter of my guide May Kim Chaw referred to the Shwedagon Pagoda, symbol of Rangoon, with some frustration, 'Why is it that only my brother can go inside?' She may be influenced by her mother who, besides having the traditional strength of Burmese women, had also absorbed a modern feminist way of thinking when she was a student in the United States.

In addition to this barrier of Buddhist thought, women suffer from the difficult socio-economic situation. In the central dry zone, around Mandalay, for example, the water shortage is very serious, and since it is women's work to fetch the water, they must carry it from the river or public sources sometimes several kilometres away, which is really hard work. Also, there are many women who suffer from diseases caused by bad sanitary conditions. The problem facing Burmese women today is not one of sex discrimination, but how to improve the quality of their lives in general.

I will always remember the gentle smiles of the Burmese women whom I met during my visit to their country. Even under harsh physical conditions, they lead lives rich in spirituality and full of vitality.

9.
Women Create a New Philippines: President Aquino and Women Power

Introduction

'A nation is not free unless its women are free' was the slogan printed on a huge wooden backdrop framing the stage in Luneta Park in the capital city of Manila on International Women's Day, 8 March 1986. Painted on the backdrop were figures of women of different races in powerful militant poses, demonstrating solidarity among women around the world. This slogan captured the enthusiasm and determination of many thousands of Filipino women who filled the park following the inauguration of President Corazon Aquino who succeeded the deposed Marcos to become the first woman President in Asia. The fever of excitement reached a high point during this rally sponsored by GABRIELA, a coalition of more than seventy Filipino women's groups.

Participants in the rally were proud that 'people power', especially 'women power', had ousted the Marcos regime of oppression and corruption that had lasted for more than twenty years. They were determined to continue their struggle with the new government until they realized true liberation. Delegates of women workers, mothers from the slums, and women peasants, one after another, appeared on the stage and gave powerful messages; each word created a stir in the audience. A thin woman from among them was greeted with thunderous applause as she lifted her right hand high and stood before the microphone. A lovely little girl toddled toward her. She took the child up in her arms and began to speak, the child resting on her right arm. This was thirty-six-year-old Judy Tagiwalo, just released from prison, and her child, two-year-old Indy who had been born in prison.

Judy made a strong appeal: 'Cory is a symbol of the Filipino woman who has fought courageously against the dictatorship, and also a symbol of the victims of harsh suppression. Let us continue to fight with Cory.'

A University of the Philippines graduate, Judy became a social worker among the poor. In 1973, the year following President Marcos's declaration of martial law, Judy was arrested in Iloilo; this was her first arrest. She was cruelly tortured; her clothes were taken away and she was left naked, sometimes forced to sit on ice. After a year and a half, she was released but rearrested in 1984 in Angeles because she refused to stop her political activities. At that time, she was seven months pregnant with Indy. She and the baby lived together in prison until her recent release. Now, after such hardships, here she was free and talking to the women gathered. Thinking of how great a sacrifice many Filipino women had to make in order to realize this moment, I could share their joy.

Judy was only one of numerous women political detainees who had courageously resisted the oppression of the Marcos years. According to a May 1985 survey, out of 645 political prisoners, 106 were women, forty of whom were mothers and seventeen of them had been arrested along with their husbands, forcing a break-up of these families since the children would have to be placed in scattered places for care. It was reported that some women were raped in prison. How much pain and agony these imprisoned women had to suffer because of their struggle for the liberation of the poor!

The large number of women detainees indicates the strength of the Filipina, for they were full participants in the fight for liberation and did not simply leave it to men.

During my first visit to Manila in 1980, I had the impression that this country is the home of courageous women. I met a number of women professors and researchers at universities and institutes. At banks, I saw many women, including managers, and women managers at hotels as well as public relations officers. In government offices, women hold positions of department chiefs or section chiefs. In the mass media, nearly half of the journalists are women. In this Roman Catholic country, many nuns are active in the fields of social welfare and education. In the markets, I saw women traders; and young factory women openly expressed their opinions. I was almost overwhelmed by this display of women power in all sectors of this society.

Compared with other Asian countries I have visited, women's participation in society is quite advanced in the Philippines. Filipino women have a strong sense of mission, and the ability to work for change in their unjust society where the gap between rich and poor is so profound. They are also imbued with a warmth that allows them to trust each other.

Economically exploited by the United States, Japan, and other First

World countries, politically oppressed by the Marcos regime and so impoverished that sixty per cent of the people earn less than 10,000 pesos (20,000 yen) per family each year, it is the women who are the most marginalized. Because of this grinding poverty, many of them have had to sell their bodies in Manila and in foreign countries, or migrate to work as maids, separated from their families; some have even become 'mail-order brides'. Women are viewed as merchandise to be used for profit. In such dire situations the Filipino women have not kept silent; they have continued to protest with great courage.

Cory Aquino

Brothers and sisters, I am grateful for the authority given to me today, and I promise to offer as much as possible to serve you. Ninoy [nickname of the assassinated opposition leader Benigno Aquino, Corazon's husband] believed that the united power of the people could overthrow such a wicked and well-organized dictator. His cruel death has resulted in this unity, this 'people power'. Citizens of my country, I appeal to you to rebuild our beautiful country together.

These words were spoken with dignity by Philippine President Cory Aquino in her February 1986 inaugural address. It was this people power, especially of countless unknown women, that propelled her to the top, to become the President of over fifty-three million Filipinos. Contrary to the expectations of professional critics both inside and outside the country, this ordinary housewife achieved an extraordinary position. I was a witness to this process of transformation.

I met Cory Aquino for the first time in 1981 when she was visiting Japan with her husband Benigno to attend a friend's wedding. He was then a political exile, and lived in the United States for medical reasons. She wore a plain brown dress and appeared to be quite an ordinary person. Even though she was constrained from making any political comments because of her husband's position, she told me about her painful ten years as the wife of a political prisoner, trying to support herself and their five children. She spoke of her shock at the death sentence imposed on her husband by the Marcos government, and how he had spent seven years and seven months in prison. She talked about her feelings of isolation because her friends and acquaintances had all abandoned her. When her husband was allowed to leave the Philippines and go to the United States for medical treatment, their family lived together in exile. 'I am just waiting for the day when we can return to our country,' she said.

Then she added, 'Ninoy is, after all, out of prison, but I am deeply concerned about political detainees who remain there, and their families. I pray also for Kim Dae-jung in South Korea to be released from prison as soon as possible. Because he has also been sentenced to death, I wrote a letter of encouragement to his wife Lee Hee-ho, as I am also a condemned criminal's wife.'

She was worried about Kim Dae-jung who was in the same position as her own husband as an opposition leader resisting a dictatorship. My impression at that time was of a rather reserved housewife, but also a person with a warm heart and a strong will.

After Benigno Aquino's assassination

I next saw Cory Aquino again in August 1983, just after the shocking assassination of Benigno Aquino in Manila. Ninoy had returned to his country saying, 'when my country is suffering, I cannot endure a comfortable life in Boston; I want to be with the Filipino people'. He said he was prepared for 'imprisonment, execution, or assassination'. Then, he was shot dead before he could take even two or three steps in his motherland. The tragedy took place on a Sunday, 21 August. In the United States, Cory heard the sad news of her husband's death, and returned to Manila with her five children on the evening of 24 August. I saw the crowds waiting for her at the airport, and saw her being caught in the crush of the press. Her face was pale with sorrow and fatigue and almost expressionless as she finally got into a car and was driven away.

Her residence in Quezon City, in the northern suburbs of Manila, was surrounded by a crowd of thousands of people. All had come to pay their last respects to Ninoy. A glass-covered coffin was placed in the centre of a small living room. Inside lay the body of Ninoy still dressed in his bloody clothes. There was a crucifix on the wall above the coffin; the hanging figure of Jesus appeared to be watching over him. The long lines of people waiting to pay tribute to a slain leader had continued without interruption, around the clock, since the day following the assassination. When Cory and the children arrived at the residence, however, the crowd was prevented from entering for some time to allow the widow and the children to bid farewell to a beloved husband and father.

Just before midnight, the children came out into the garden where the press was waiting, and then Cory appeared. Dressed in black and carrying a white handkerchief she said:

Just now I have kissed Ninoy, and as I was gazing at him it was as if he was smiling at me. I said to my daughters, 'Papa is smiling at us, isn't he?' Now I am convinced that people really love Ninoy; I believe that his death was not useless, and his return here was right . . . Ninoy was a person of non-violence, of peace, of courage. I will follow this way of living too.

Even though her beloved husband was dead, she contained her sorrow and remained calm. With awe-inspiring control, she spoke clearly about the meaning of her husband's death, and her own future. From time to time, in the cool dark of the garden at midnight, one could see tears caught in the glare of TV camera lights, running down her cheeks. She looked so determined, so strong-willed, to achieve the unfinished tasks of her husband.

My third meeting with her took place one year later in September 1984, at her office in the Cojuangco Building in Manila. In those days, outraged by the assassination of Benigno Aquino, the Filipino people, from slum dwellers and workers to the middle classes of the Makati business centre and residential areas, all participated in demonstrations demanding the resignation of Marcos; the democratizing movement against the dictatorial regime was intensifying. Cory was always a participant; she became a symbol as a victim of oppression as well as a symbol of those who were fighting against it. 'I promised Ninoy that I would do anything in order to restore democracy in the Philippines.' She did not hide her determination to fight without wavering.

On this day, she wore a blue dress and seemed to have gained a little weight. She had changed from a sorrowful widow in mourning to a militant activist. Surrounded by women supporters, she looked relaxed, and commented to me, a Japanese, 'I have been to Cebu Island; it seems that the sex tours have moved from Manila to Cebu, haven't they?' I realized then that she had a woman's point of view.

A year and a half later, in early March 1986, I had a chance to meet President Aquino just after her inauguration. I was covering the visit of Takako Doi, Chairperson of the Japan Socialist Party, the major opposition party, who had come to congratulate the new President, her long-time friend. We went to the Cojuangco Building office, as this occasion was before the move to the Malacañang Palace. Located in the Makati district, the building was surrounded by a large crowd of people, supporters and those who expected much from the new President. The streets were filled with the symbolic yellow colour, and 'people power' placards filled the area. The enthusiasm of the people who would bring about a new Philippines by ousting the Marcos regime was still high. Many women were busy at the entrance, and in the elevators, and even in the President's office. The atmosphere was typical of a woman's office, warm and informal.

On this occasion, President Aquino wore a short-sleeved dress of yellow – her symbol colour – with a neat and pretty white lace collar. Pushed into the campaign by a million signatures, she appeared dauntless and toughened by a campaign that had taken her through sixty-eight provinces, more than any other candidate. She had survived more than forty days of sometimes very intense campaigning, and had caught a cold, probably because of exhaustion. But, once she began to speak, it was clear that she had already acquired the dignity of her office.

> Seventy per cent of the people in our country live in poverty as they are unemployed or only partially employed. The most urgent task is to solve this economic crisis in order to bring stability to the lives of the Filipino people, to restore their rights and their freedoms. We ask for economic aid useful for the people in rural development and health care. Until now, Japan's economic aid has not been used for the poor in our country, therefore, I will have to review this. Since our new government is pledged to work for the people, we will use Japan's aid properly, not as before.

She talked frankly with her old friend Takako Doi, and discussed the difficulties she was facing as President because she knew that even though political change had been achieved, the necessary economic reconstruction would not be easy. During the short twenty-minute interview, she repeatedly used the words 'the poor'.

From housewife to President

Born in Manila in January 1933, Corazon's father, José Cojuangco, was a former senator and a wealthy landlord of a 6,000-hectare sugar-cane plantation in the province of Talrac in central Luzon. A daughter of one of the richest families in the Philippines, at the age of twelve she was sent to the United States for her education. She later entered a women's college in New York where she studied French and mathematics. During her student days she met Benigno Aquino, son of a famous family of politicans from the same province of Talrac; they were married in 1954 when Ninoy was twenty-two and Cory was twenty-one.

The year following their marriage, Ninoy was elected mayor of their residential town; at twenty-eight, state governor; at thirty-four, senator; and at thirty-eight, presidential candidate of the Liberal Party. He forged a brilliant career as a politician; Cory devoted herself to bringing up their five children. She chose the low-profile role of a supportive wife to a politician.

In 1972, President Marcos declared martial law and arrested Benigno Aquino, his most powerful rival, on charges of plotting to overthrow the government and treason. This development caused a drastic change in Cory's happy life. Her husband was imprisoned for more than seven years and, in 1977, a military court sentenced him to death. Imprisonment, a capital sentence, exile, and, finally, assassination – she shared her husband's tragic latter half of life. Through such an ordeal, this daughter of a millionaire came to know the pain of oppressed people, and thus, in spite of her class, began to identify with the poor.

Her administration was composed mostly of a mixture of the military, old politicians, and business leaders. Even the leftist nationalist group Bayan, and others who wanted more radical changes, supported her because they reasoned that, 'President Aquino should not be isolated in this administration because she needs support and identification with the grass-roots.'

She said to Ninoy's mother Aurora, 'The only thing I can give to the people is sincerity and the determination to clean up politics.' This kind of sincerity may have gained support regardless of political opinion. Even if she is unable to achieve true socio-economic structural change, such as land reform, and if her role is over when the people who have struggled for change become strong enough, her contribution to history in ousting a dictator and ushering in a new Philippines will never be erased.

I said 'yes' to a million signatures that asked me to run; the 'people power' phenomenon began and rallied round the widow of Ninoy. The people are crying for change. Even the poorest offered gestures of support. And the women! They have cast caution to the winds to campaign and lead in the people's crusade. They are determined to prove that people power is mightier than all the men and money of the crumbling dictatorship. I have heard the anguished voices of the victims of injustice. I have been kissed by the poorest of the poor, and have felt the warmth of their tears on my cheeks.

This is a speech that Candidate Aquino made a few days before the election. She campaigned for election with the steadfast decision to be on the side of the poor and of the women who were suffering under the Marcos administration. And she won.

From housewife to widow, to fighter, and finally, to President, Cory Aquino has experienced such dramatic changes in her life. I clearly remember her face as I had seen it at each stage. This remarkable transformation in one life lends credence to the potential of her country's transformation from suffering to liberation.

'No matter how long the night, dawn will surely come.' These words by priest, poet, and political prisoner Ed de la Torre express the hope and longing for the dawn of political detainees in his country. I was deeply impressed by the role women played in bringing in this long-awaited dawn. In their demonstrations for Aquino, shabbily dressed women wore small badges pinned to their breasts, 'Cory is my President'. It was an expression of strong expectations of a woman president from poor people.

Mita Tavera, woman minister

I am very glad to have Mamita as Minister of Social Welfare and Development in my cabinet. She has been devoted to grass-roots activities. Please ask her about our needs for Japanese government development aid.

When President Aquino mentioned the name 'Mamita', Takako Doi looked very happy. Mamita is the nickname of woman doctor Mita Tavera. I though this cabinet appointment a good concrete example of Aquino's oft-stated intent to be 'on the side of the poor people'.

It was through an anti sex-tour campaign that I became acquainted with Dr Tavera. In January 1981, when Japan's former Prime Minister Zenko Suzuki visited Manila, Mamita was one of the organizers of a Filipino women's protest action against Japanese men's prostitution tourism. She shared her story with me:

I live near the Japanese-owned Manila Garden Hotel where many Japanese tourists stay, and I was saddened by the behaviour of the Japanese men. Women of poor developing countries are exploited as cheap labour by rich countries or used as sex objects by rich men; but we are unable to express our outrage under this dictatorship. We will never accept this situation; it is a question of human dignity. We cannot keep silent any longer and we have decided to speak out.

The protest rally was held at St Paul's Women's College near Mabini, a tourist district in Manila.

> If Prime Minister Suzuki wants to promote friendly relations with ASEAN [Association of South East Asian Nations] countries, he might also remember to promote friendly relations between people. Unless he stops this sex tourism, he cannot establish friendly relationships.

This strong speech was made by Dr Tavera without any of her usual smiles.

When she mentioned the word 'people', it carried a lot of weight because she herself was known as a doctor trying to serve people at the grass-roots level. Her Spanish blood gives her a fair skin and tall stature, and from her appearance it is clear that she comes from a rich family background. Her father was a banker and her grandfather was a friend of José Rizal, a hero in Philippine history.

> Since I was a young girl, I wanted to have a job that would help people so I decided to study medicine. During World War Two the Japanese army came to the Philippines and my house was burned down; many of my friends were killed. But still I was able to graduate from the university, and I was engaged in medical research for three years. After the war, I decided to make my contribution to eradicate tuberculosis.

In those days, many poor people had tuberculosis and died, one after another; few doctors wanted to specialize in its treatment. Dr Tavera, who had chosen medical work in order to help poor people, volunteered to be a specialist in tubercular treatment, and joined the Philippine Tuberculosis Society. Later, she became the Executive Director and a pioneer in the campaign to rid the country of this disease.

In 1972, President Marcos declared martial law, and Dr Tavera was considered a subversive element because of her attitude in her work to the people she was treating. In 1974, she was expelled from the Society where she had worked for thirty years because of pressure from the Marcos government. She was not deterred by this persecution. 'I can never give up my most important task of combating poverty.' She then organized a People's Health Movement (AKAP), and started campaigning to teach poor people themselves how to protect their health.

Rural health education

In 1981, I visited the AKAP headquarters in the northern suburbs of Manila. There were piles of pamphlets on the office shelves. Dr Tavera took several and, turning the pages, said, 'There are many illiterate mothers in the rural villages so that's why many pictures and illustrations are used in these booklets. These are guidebooks for mothers on how to give first aid to their children when they have fevers or when they get hurt.'

AKAP had thirty paid staff and more than 100 volunteer workers who devoted themselves to rural health care in fourteen provinces.

> Many children die without ever seeing a doctor. We have done research on how to make drugs using local materials, and we teach people how to make medicines from leaves or grasses growing in their neighbourhoods.

Dr Tavera showed me several rolls of white cloth on which pictures were painted. The health workers carry these rolls for presentation to the villagers outdoors, even when it is raining; this is why cloth is used rather than paper.

Next, I was shown slides illustrating activities in rural villages. Village people are so poor that they often die from such common illnesses as diarrhoea or colds, because they have no medicine, neither do they eat nutritious food. One picture showed a sad-faced, young mother sitting in front of a makeshift farmhouse embracing her sick child.

Dr Tavera, who sees health care as part of the liberation movement, said: 'The death rate due to malnutrition, tuberculosis, and malaria is very high. These health problems are directly related to poverty. Our health activity is a struggle against poverty'.

AKAP was also making efforts in health activities in slum areas in Manila. Squatters, pushed out of poor rural villages, come to Manila. With no place to live, they have to construct some kind of shelter so they put up small huts with pieces of discarded wood found along the seashore or on the river banks. One-third of the inhabitants of Manila live in such slums. 'If they have clean and safe drinking water, seventy percent of children under five years old who are dying from diarrhoea can be saved.' Each time Dr Tavera visits one of these slums, she grieves that young lives are lost in this unhealthy environment; there is no piped water nor even lavatories. She is also pained by the sight of the young women going out to the red-light districts in order to support their poor families. 'It is my task to help the people to stand up, to take action for improving their living conditions through my health activities.' She is struggling not only as a doctor, but also as a social activist.

In March 1986, I visited Dr Tavera at home in Manila's high-class residential area.

> We have no more dictator. I feel so free, just like a bird. During the Marcos years, those of us who were engaged in grass-roots activities were suspect, so we were always afraid because we didn't know when we might be arrested. But now, the President herself wants to be a part of the grass-roots people.

After many years of difficulty and hardships, Dr Tavera expressed her joy with her whole body. I felt then, this is really the joy of life.

Her feelings however, did not prevent her understanding the difficulties of economic reconstruction facing the new government.

> It is only the beginning of a long process. From now on we will have to sacrifice ourselves in a way different from in the Marcos period. Our country has a huge foreign debt, US$35 billion, and Marcos took several billion dollars with him when he left. Of course the people are impoverished, even in such a rich country; we need a clean and honest government.

Dr Tavera was recommended for the job of minister in the Aquino administration by a Catholic group interested in social welfare, as well as by other women's groups. She thought it necessary to show support for a President who was trying to maintain a clean and honest political environment, and she organized a women's demonstration to emphasize this support. The result was a sea of women dressed in yellow filling Manila's main street, Taft Street. They were carrying banners and placards with slogans in Tagalog, such as 'Women's Power', and 'Long Live Women', 'Women's Victory' and so on, and Dr Tavera walked at the head of this long line of marchers. She had previously participated in anti-Marcos demonstrations on many occasions after Benigno Aquino's assassination, but this time she led the demonstration of victory as a member of the newly elected government. She was surrounded by young nurses, and her smile conveyed warmth and modesty, common characteristics of the Filipina.

Sister Christine Tan

In March 1986, on the same day as my visit with Takako Doi to President Aquino's office, I was present at a party one evening in honour of Ninoy's mother Aurora's seventy-sixth birthday. The President came to the party directly from her office and was seated at the main table. Beside her sat a Catholic nun in a cotton blouse and a grey head covering – Christine Tan – close friend and personal advisor to President Aquino. She looked calm and thoughtful as usual, watching the people who came to greet the President, and speaking with her from time to time.

I first met Sister Tan through the campaign against sex tourism in 1977, when I attended the Asian Women's Forum in Penang, Malaysia. I remember being very impressed by this militant nun who is devoted to social welfare activities. We met again in 1980 at the Christian Conference of Asia's International Workshop on Tourism in Manila.

During that time spent in Manila, I was shocked by the disgusting situation in the hotels filled with Japanese male tourists, and I wanted to see the red-light districts at night. It was arranged that Sister Tan would escort me. I waited that evening at a seafood restaurant on Loxas Boulevard. I was surprised when she arrived dressed in a flower-print dress instead of her nun's habit. She said, 'I am in disguise because I am a wanted person.' She took me to bars and gogo clubs, but she was very careful and always kept her head down.

It was still early in the evening when we saw inside one dark and empty bar. Young women in bareback dresses were sitting idly at the counter waiting for customers. When Sister Tan spoke with them they were open and very friendly. Most of them were fifteen or sixteen years old, coming from the islands of Visayas, an economically depressed region. Their common need as expressed to us was 'I want to have friends.' Though their home villages were poor, they had been raised in an atmosphere of warm human relations within large families and in the city they were lonely, limited as they were to commercial transactions with strangers. This is why, when approached by a sympathetic person like Sister Tan, such girls are eager to talk to her.

I had a glimpse into another gogo bar where, amid an explosion of sound, semi-nude women were dancing on a stage. Men were seated around a dark counter circling the stage, choosing which bodies to buy – merely items on sale at a flesh market.

Since then I have visited such places in most Asian countries, and talked with the women there, but this visit with Sister Tan was my first experience of seeing women as merchandise. It was so shocking that I can never forget it. These women are human beings as we all are, but they have no means of survival other than as objects to satisfy the sexual desires of foreign men. At the same time, there are people who make huge profits by using them in this way. I was terrified by this inhuman situation in our modern society.

'This is a problem of human dignity,' Sister Tan murmured, as if she could imagine what was in my mind, and she led me away from the streets of glittering neon. We walked quietly in the dark lanes feeling the breath of warm tropical breezes, and the sounds of moving palm branches covered our silence. After about a fifteen-minute walk, we were in a narrow alley lined with foul-smelling drainage ditches. She opened a small wooden door and I could see a drab and shabby house beyond a small open space where laundry was hanging. 'This is our house,' she said. We were in the Leveliza slum area, and this town is a symbol of endemic poverty where 35,000 families live crowded together amid the garbage and the stink. Sister Tan told me:

> I feel angry, when I can see from here those tall luxurious 5-star hotels. It is in those hotels that men enjoy their nights with young innocent girls. Many of them are Japanese tourists. Both those men and these people who live in this slum are human beings, aren't they? This is the place where you can so clearly see the unfair relationship between those from the rich and those from the poor countries.

Living in the slums

Four years later, in 1984, I met Sister Tan again; she was still living in the same slum.

> I want to live with the poor people who are, after all, eighty percent of our population. I borrowed this shabby house for one year in 1979, and now I have been living here for six years. I am completely accustomed to a life where I lie down on the floor and sleep. Sometimes I am bitten by rats.

She seemed unperturbed by such an unpleasant life for herself but said:

> It is very painful to hear children, babies, crying at night because of their hunger, or mothers trying to hush them up. Some mothers have mental problems because of the stress of worrying about feeding their children. . . . Recently, a baby boy was found dead in

a shoebox. Economic crises hit the poor people at the bottom hardest.

Because she is so eager to help her poor neighbours, she is always busy running here and there raising funds to buy rice or collecting used clothing. Sister Tan was born and brought up in a wealthy Chinese family. Her father was a judge and later became a banker. According to her, he was a man with a sense of justice, and her mother was always concerned about poor people. She was the fifth child in a loving family of seven children.

When she was thirteen years old, she contracted tuberculosis and was obliged to spend the next five years in bed. Finally, she made up her mind to be a Catholic nun and lead a life of service, so she entered a Catholic women's college. 'I was brought up in a happy family, and I wanted to share this happiness with others.' After graduation, she worked as a social worker for one year in a poor area in Los Angeles in the United States. On her return, she joined the Good Shepherd Convent, an order zealous in social welfare activities for the poor. At that time, she was twenty-three years old.

Outstanding in various activities as a teacher and social worker, Sister Tan was greatly respected and, in 1972, just before the declaration of martial law, she was elected head of an association of 9,000 nuns from sixty-five convents throughout the Philippines.

Sister Tan recalled that:

On the day following the beginning of martial law, the sisters' association had a meeting, and we were the first to issue a statement protesting against the immorality of martial law. One step further; then the next step after that. We took protest actions, first one, then another.

The nuns reacted to the martial law situation before the priests did, which is a reflection of the strength of the Filipino women in religious circles. In a Catholic country like the Philippines, the social influence of the nuns is far stronger than the Japanese – or people in the West – can imagine. Sister Tan, from her position of leadership, carried a sense of resistance to oppression from the people's point of view, which was very effective.

Under martial law, oppression became increasingly violent, and many people were victimized, imprisoned, tortured, and murdered. At the risk of personal danger, Sister Tan devoted herself to human rights activities for political detainees. 'I needed courage and firm documented evidence.' Once, she was placed on a 'subversive elements' list for some time as a wanted criminal, but she never gave up these efforts, even working under extremely difficult and dangerous conditions.

It was Sister Tan who gave encouragement to Benigno Aquino and his family when he was imprisoned under a death sentence. As she was busy about her work she thought, 'To preach about poverty and hunger, or social justice and human rights, from the comfortable chair of presidency of the nun's association was a contradiction, and I couldn't stand it any longer.' In 1976, when her term as president ended, she began to search for a new lifestyle, and for enrichment to her spiritual life.

Having heard about Zen Buddhism from a Vietnamese nun, and wanting to learn more about it, she went to Kamakura, Japan, where she took religious training in a temple.

> Money, honour, power, knowledge – all these things are meaningless, just like bubbles. That's what I felt. I could understand the oriental spirituality that is so different from the Western way of thinking, a way that insists too strongly on the ego.

Sister Tan was broadminded about learning from other religions.

> Her spirituality was deepened by her Zen training, and she made it the base of her social practice.

> True Buddhism teaches a lifestyle that answers to all the agonies of this world. In Japan where there is material prosperity and a comfortable life, Buddhism can sleep, but in the Philippines, we have much to do. I must live with the eighty percent of my people who are poor.

After three years of spiritual growth, in 1979 she decided to move to the slum. She rises at four o'clock in the morning for about an hour of private meditation; at six o'clock, she and the three nuns who share her house celebrate mass together. After breakfast, she commutes to the Catholic Center for Social Concerns in Santa Mesa, and spends the whole day moving from one thing to the next. She comes home very late at night and goes to sleep after evening prayers.

Support for Cory

Sister Tan's life became even busier after the assassination of Benigno Aquino in 1983. When Cory returned from the United States with her children, Sister Tan was there to give comfort and encouragement, more so than any other person. During this period, Sister Tan was also extremely busy as one of the leaders of the anti-government movement that had intensified all around the country with the slogan, 'Let's not waste Ninoy's death; let's overthrow the Marcos regime.'

In autumn 1984, I was waiting at the airport for a flight to Cebu Island when, much to my surprise, I ran into Sister Tan dressed in her usual habit of blue skirt and grey head covering. Normally, she would have been participating in a demonstration in Manila, but today she was on her way to organize some rural groups for action. I asked her:

When do you think Marcos will be overthrown? Already a year has passed since Aquino's assassination and numerous demonstrations have been held, but the Marcos regime has not yet been toppled.

Not the least bit disconcerted by this rather provocative question she answered:

We shouldn't be in a hurry. Time is needed for consciousness-raising among as many people as possible. Just to change from Marcos to another ruler is not a true change. Not only by demonstrations, but also by economic boycott, non-payment of taxes, and all other possible non-violent means, people should be empowered. Sooner or later Marcos will fall. We don't want to rush this. Don't be frustrated. . . .

Under martial law, there was nothing but dictatorship or communism, but since Aquino's assassination, the vacuum between these two extremes has been filled by an awakened people power. People who fervently aspired to a free Philippines, liberated from dictatorship and foreign dominance, are standing up and taking action.

One and a half years after this conversation, in February 1986, people power finally ousted Marcos without bloodshed. It was a victory for the people, and it was their support that put Cory Aquino in the position of President.

Sister Tan, however, continued to live in Leveliza slum, helping poor people find jobs and, at the same time, encouraging President

Aquino as a close friend and advisor. One of the first measures taken by Cory Aquino as President was to order the release of political prisoners, including leaders of the Philippine Communist Party and the New Peoples Army, defying the wishes of the military. This courageous decision was urged on her not only by her own painful experiences as a political prisoner's wife, but also on the advice of Sister Tan who had worked hard for a very long time for the sake of many of these prisoners. 'The release of political prisoners is necessary from a humanitarian standpoint, and it is also politically vital. If the Aquino government wants to build a new Philippines, the President must co-operate with everyone, even with communists,' Sister Tan said.

I was suddenly reminded of a scene in the garden of Aquino's residence several days after Ninoy's assassination. Cory had appeared before the press and demanded, 'If Mr Marcos wants to express his condolences to my family, he can do so by releasing all political prisoners.' Sister Tan was sitting calmly beside her and gave a supplementary report on the situation of political prisoners to the gathered press. Two and a half years had passed since that day and Cory herself was able to fulfil this demand.

Almost immediately after the President's office was moved into Malacañang Palace, slum dwellers were invited to come and see it for themselves. Sister Tan had arranged this. Her strong wish was that this woman President, born and raised in a wealthy family and, after many years of suffering reaching the pinnacle of power in this country, might be able to maintain the political stance of giving the highest priority to the restoration of human rights to the most oppressed people at the bottom.

'What suffering people in Asia want is not compassion, or lamentation, or tears, or even prayers. They want anger.' This is a well-known comment from Sister Tan. She is a woman of tender heart, but she is called 'Angry Sister'. This anger was directed toward the Marcos government, and to Japan who supported it. 'If Japan wants to help us, please stop interfering; please keep away from the sea, the rivers, the forests, and the brothels of the Philippines.' This is the anger that exploded and brought about a new Philippines. 'Still today, people are suffering from poverty. Please help us with that traditional Asian kindness, and human sympathy,' said Sister Tan. It cannot be denied that Japan has some responsibility for increasing and prolonging the suffering of the people in this country. This is why I, a Japanese, took her comments very seriously.

A woman of deep religious spirituality and courageous action, she personifies the power of the Filipina. 'Women gained the victory. It was the women who stood before the tanks. I was there too; I shall never forget that day.' Sister Tan spoke with pride as she told me about the bloodless Filipino revolution that took place on 25 February 1986.

'I was frightened in front of the tanks, and I almost wanted to run away, but I stayed because the Catholic sisters stood firm without moving. Women were braver; women brought about the victory.' This is how Ninoy's brother Agapito Aquino described his experience on that day of revolution.

It was really the grass-roots women, the mothers in the slums, and the young women workers, who were not afraid of the tanks. It is these women who, along with President Cory Aquino and her friends Dr Tavera and Sister Tan, created a new Philippines.

10.
Korean Women for Democratization: The Mothers' Courageous Struggle

Introduction

'My Mother's Name is Worry'

In summer, my mother worries about water;
In winter, she worries about coal briquettes,
And all year long, she worries about rice.

In daytime, my mother worries about living;
At night, she worries about the children,
And all day long, she worries and worries.

This is why my mother's name is 'worry'.
My father's name is 'drunken frenzy',
And my name is 'tears and sighs'.

(Written by a twelve-year-old girl living in the slums of South Korea.)

Concluding my assignment as Asia Correspondent for the *Asahi Shimbun*, I stopped over in South Korea on my way back to Japan. Along with Taiwan, Hong Kong and Singapore South Korea is known as one of the newly industrialized countries; together, these particular places are known as the 'four dragons of East Asia'. I saw evidence of the capital city Seoul participating in South Korea's dynamic economic development; newly built high-rise buildings and apartments gave a lively atmosphere to a city preparing for the 1988 Olympic Games. At the same time, however, it was also clear that the slums had been excluded from this economic prosperity and were expanding to the point of explosion. The poem quoted above succinctly describes the situation of poor mothers who live in these areas.

Slum dwellers and elite women

In order to help alleviate some of the problems of women in the slums, thirty-one-year-old Hong Min lives in the Mansok-Dong slum in the city of Inchon, a port city west of Seoul. Wearing track-suit trousers, she greeted me and guided me to a wooden house with a sign at the entrance: 'Big Water School Children's Center'.

Mothers in the slums usually go out to work so the children are virtually abandoned after they return from school. Quite a number of them drop out and are drawn into juvenile delinquency. This is why I started school children's care. We help them do their homework and give them some cultural education with drama or slides. Every day, seventy to eighty children come here.

The room was rather empty when I visited because the children had already gone home, and a variety of colourful pictures were hanging on the wall. 'This centre was opened in February 1984. Now I leave the work here to a young woman graduate of Seoul National University. I myself am trying to organize the mothers.' Hong Min walked with light and experienced steps through the dark lanes flooded with waste water.

We visited a little house where two women sat in a small three-metre-square room that had Korean-style floor heating. The younger woman was a healer, who had been trained as a nurse, and whose present livelihood was to provide traditional medical treatment to the people in the slum. Those who could not afford to see a doctor were dependent on her treatment. On this evening, she was massaging the back of a middle-aged woman who was suffering from anaemia.

She was a cheerful person, fond of Japanese popular songs, and a very good friend of Hong Min. Together, they were engaged in education programmes for the mothers on family planning, child bearing, and education of children. Hong Min pointed out, 'There are many mothers here who suffer not only from physical illnesses but also mental problems and worries because of their poverty. Just talking with them is an encouragement.' Hong Min had been counselling with the woman who had anaemia, because she is also an abused wife.

Mansok-Dong slum was a red-light district during the Japanese colonial period, but during the Korean War a number of refugees from North Korea settled here. It is said that in Seoul there are more than 200 slum areas, accommodating one out of every four or five citizens, due to migration to the city from the poverty-stricken rural areas.

Mansok-Dong differs slightly from other slums because of its thirty-year history, but the environment of about 800 families (4–5,000 people) living here is no less dreadful than in the other slums. There are only eight filthy and inconveniently placed toilets for common use. Electricity is available in this district, but many families cannot afford it and use candles instead. Hong Min told me that:

> The men here are mostly fishermen or unstable seasonal workers with meagre incomes, and most are unemployed. Therefore, the women have to work. Some catch shell-fish, some are pedlars, and others do piece-work at home to earn a little extra money. Some women work at the nearby furniture factory, but their salary is only about 130,000 *won* per month [about 30,000 yen], which is only half of what the men workers earn. Really, such a miserable life!

Such poverty and despair cause typical social problems: juvenile delinquency, such as theft; family violence; injuries; labour accidents; disease, and so forth. There are no social welfare activities planned here, probably because it is such an old slum and largely ignored.

'I heard about the situation here from a friend who lives nearby, and made up my mind to live here and try to do something about it.' Hong Min told me about her own life in a matchbox-size house at the end of a small, smelly alley. Her husband is a businessman, and they have two children, aged five and seven. It was not easy for her to become a slum worker.

> In January last year, I moved here by myself, leaving my family in Seoul, because if I commute I will not be trusted by the people here. My husband was strongly against my plan, of course, and this crisis nearly caused a divorce. But I persuaded him so earnestly that finally he reluctantly agreed to move here with our children. Now he commutes to his office from here.

It is taken for granted that a wife will follow her husband when he chooses to act on his idealism, but such a reversal as this is rare in any country. I was impressed by her courageous decision and enthusiasm that gained her the co-operation of her husband.

What was it that drew her into such activities? She was raised in a wealthy family and had studied sociology at the prestigious Ewha Women's University.

> I got married, was raising my children, living with my mother-in-

law, and also had a job, but it was not easy to do all those things even though my family was financially well off. I thought then how difficult life must be for women in poor families. I was doing educational activities for middle-class housewives, and I felt a kind of emptiness. This is why I decided that my role is to work at consciousness-raising for women at the bottom of society.

At that time, a new feminist group, Women for Equality and Peace, was just being organized and she became a member. This group supported her activities by adopting the slum work as a project and formed a special fund-raising committee.

Hong Min began with the centre for school children, then opened a literacy class for mothers; she began to counsel on problems related to health and child care. After this, she worked on workers' accident compensation for those involved in factory accidents, all the while busily moving around in the slum.

It took some time to establish close relationships, to get the people to open their hearts to me, because I was brought up in a middle-class family where even the way of speaking and sense of life or culture are all different. Women in the slums have been oppressed for so long that they can't speak up. They have little confidence in solving their problems by themselves, and are too dependent on someone else. In order to increase the numbers of independent women who can act for themselves, I patiently try to establish a relationship of mutual trust.

She was equally frank about the difficulties of her work:

Now my urgent task is to organize women to fight against slum eviction. In poor families, women have to take responsibility when they are still young. That's why women are more reliable than men at critical times.

Hong Min is a determined worker, convinced that women have great potentiality.

Not only Hong Min, but also many other women are turning their backs on a happy and carefree life in Seoul to try to live among and serve the poor people in the shabby, makeshift houses in the slums. The Serve the People movement is quietly expanding. This is a movement of students and graduates of such first-class universities as Seoul National, Yonsei, Ewha; concealing their educated backgrounds these students become factory workers.

> I think about a thousand of them are already working at factories
> with the intent to live their whole lives as workers. For more than
> ten years those young people, made aware through the student
> movement, have chosen this lifestyle and quietly devoted
> themselves to consciousness-raising and organizing workers.

These are the words of Lee Oo-chung, a theologian who was dismissed
from Seoul Women's University, committed to human rights activities
such as helping the families of political detainees. She herself has
experienced prison and torture and is widely respected as a symbol of
the movement for democracy in South Korea.

> It is not only the intellectual class who try to identify with the
> people; women workers and peasant women too have begun to
> speak up. Even the mothers of the slums come to the busy
> downtown streets to join in demonstrations against slum evictions. I
> feel that history is moving forward.

As Chairperson of the Federation of Women's Organizations,
composed of twenty different groups, Professor Lee was very happy
about the new awareness of poor women. In Korea, the distance
between the intellectual class and others has existed since the Yi
dynasty (1388–1910), a time when the country was ruled by the
yangban, or intellectual class. Besides such historical reasons, the gap
between the rich and the poor is widening because of economic
development that is not touching the poor. Both the elite's new
attitude of identifying with the common people, and the increasing
prominence of the people's voices and actions are of great significance.

Lee So-sun, 'Mother of Workers'

This new awareness on the part of grass-roots people referred to by
Professor Lee is exemplified in the person of Lee So-sun, a poor slum
mother now well known as the 'mother of Korean workers'. She is the
mother of Chun Tae-il, a twenty-two-year-old youth who worked in a
garment factory in Seoul's Peace Market, and who burned himself to
death in November 1970. To help support his poor family, this young
man started working when he was only eight years old, selling
brushes, baskets, and newspapers. He finished primary and junior high

school at night, and became a worker in the Peace Market when he was seventeen. It pained him to see the plight of young girls, aged twelve to fifteen, working as assistants to the workers in the same factory; they were brutally abused and one after another contracted tuberculosis. Chun Tae-il thought it essential to organize a labour union to improve working conditions and, because of his petition to the authorities on this matter, he was fired. But he did not give up, moving busily about to organize the workers. Finally, on 13 November 1970, about 500 Peace Market workers were mobilized and ready to march, carrying placards declaring, 'We are not machines!' The police stopped the demonstrators, but Chun Tae-il was determined to protest with the sacrifice of his life. 'Protect young women workers', he shouted as he set himself alight. He was taken to the hospital where his mother reached him in time to hear his last words, an appeal to her, 'Don't waste my death. Please be mother of the workers.' Lee So-sun's life was changed from that moment.

Born in a poor village, she has experienced every hardship. To support her drunken husband and four children she has worked as a pedlar, a domestic servant, a day labourer, and even been reduced to begging. Now, faced with her son's painful death she joined the struggle according to his wishes. He had written in his diary, 'If I had a friend among the university students, how helpful it might be.' Students who heard about this hurried to his mother's side and took up the cause. Finally, Lee So-sun succeeded in organizing the Chonggye Garment Labour Union in the Peace Market. She also was able to open a school there for the workers to help them learn their rights and to stand up and fight for these rights. Consequently, she was constantly harassed by the Minister of Labour and market employers, and arrested many times by the police. Each time she used all available means to resist, such as hunger strikes and sit-ins. She was repeatedly imprisoned.

On the fifth anniversary of her son's death, in 1975, she made a long and moving speech: 'My Labour Movement – How It Started'. In the course of this speech she said:

> Since that time [her son's death], I have struggled to keep my promise to my deceased son, and to achieve his dream. That is, to remove all of your pains as workers so that you can live as human beings. Ever since making up my mind to devote my life to the workers, I have been running around like a mad woman!

Her undaunted efforts continue. She has supported the families of political detainees; she has stood with lines of resisters confronting the riot police outside courtroom buildings during the trials of democracy-movement activists. In April 1975, eight persons belonging to the so-called People's Revolutionary Party were executed. This was widely believed to be as a result of a frame-up on the part of the government. Lee So-sun joined in a demonstration with the families of those executed, lying down in front of the police caravan carrying the bodies. She was trampled, dragged by the hair, and beaten with batons over her whole body as she was arrested.

In 1977, she was again arrested and charged with contempt of court, and the workers' school was closed. The official reason for this was that she had appeared at the trial of Chang Ki-pyo, a Seoul National University student who, among others, had responded to Chun Tae-il's death by supporting Lee So-sun in organizing the labour union movement, and had been arrested. At his trial, Lee So-sun accused the prosecutor of wilful injustice, showing the scars that she had received at the hands of the authorities. But the real reason for her arrest was because she had taken to the streets in a courageous protest action against the death of a worker who had been suffocated by poison gas at a leather factory. The authorities were fearful of rising labour conflict and again put her in gaol.

The workers in the Peace Market were angry because their mother had been taken away and their school was closed. As many as 1,000 women workers massed at the court building and shouted, 'Give us back our mother'. For those in power, Lee So-sun was a dangerous person who must be imprisoned, but this same person, a poor mother, was also a symbol of struggle against oppression for millions of workers.

When I visited South Korea in July 1981, she was once more in prison. This time she was charged with a protest action against the order to dissolve the Chonggye Garment Labour Union, founded in honour of the sacrifice of her son. This union had taken the lead in the Korean labour movement in the 1970s as the heart of a very few militant democratic unions among the vast majority of 'yellow', or pro-government unions. Lee So-sun was determined to prevent this break-up of the union, and she and more than twenty other union members appealed to the chairman of the Asia–Africa Labor Organization who was visiting Seoul at that time. Refused an interview, they occupied the office of the organization, and were all arrested by riot police called in to quell the disturbance. Chun Tae-sam, Tae-il's younger brother, was detained along with his mother. She received a sentence of ten months' hard labour.

The office of the Human Rights Committee of the Korean Council of Churches is located on the seventh floor of the Christian Broadcasting Building in central Seoul. I tried not to be noticed by the government agents watching the corridors as I slipped into the room. After a short wait, a slim young woman, simply dressed in T-shirt and jeans, entered. This was Chun Sun-ok, daughter of Lee So-sun, who had been detained for a week because she had brought an appeal to the court for the eleven union members, including her mother, who had been arrested. 'We cannot sit back and allow the rights obtained at the cost of a life be lost. All of the families are determined to share the pain in unity with the husbands, brothers, and sisters who have to fight.' This young woman was struggling bravely in place of her mother and brother in prison.

Chun Sun-ok had just returned from a visit with her mother. 'My mother is in a big cell with twenty other prisoners and she is in very high spirits. She is trying to influence those women, cell mates who have committed all sorts of crimes, to believe in some religious faith.' Clearly, Chun Sun-ok respected and trusted her mother. Lee So-sun, by sharing spiritual food with them, was trying to encourage these women who, like her, suffered at the bottom of society, and who had become criminals. It was at this point I realized that Lee So-sun's unyielding spirit and overwhelming affection was rooted in her faith. I was told that her favourite hymn is 'The Way to Heaven':

> The bright way to heaven is open before me;
> No matter how much sorrow and pains we have,
> The bright sky of the glory of heaven breaks through the darkness;
> By the blessing of the Lord,
> I am always looking at the light.

The life of Lee So-sun has truly been a painful struggle in search of light in the darkness. A poor, uneducated woman, brought to consciousness of oppression by her son's death, she became a militant fighter, afraid of neither imprisonment nor torture. Urging other sons and daughters to join the struggle to claim their rights as human beings, she is now loved as the mother of Korean workers.

> Let's fight with determination to stand up to death rather than kneel to live. Those who are ready to risk their own life for the struggle will surely win the victory; but those who shrink from the struggle will surely die.

Lee So-sun's powerful message is an inspiration for poor workers. Her supporters in Korea and abroad, moved by her brave battle, have contributed to building the Chun Tae-il Memorial Hall in Seoul, which has become the base for her activities. In the summer of 1986 she was sentenced to one and a half years' hard labour.

During 1986, a number of students emulating Chun Tae-il burned themselves in political protests, shouting, 'Down with dictatorship', and 'Guarantee the three labour rights'. Their mothers formed an Association of Families of the Democratic Movement, and Lee So-sun was elected president, even though she was in prison. These mothers pledged themselves to carry on their sons' struggles.

Families of the victims of the Kwangju Uprising

In 1980, just ten years after the death of Lee So-sun's son, a number of mothers lost their sons in the Kwangju Uprising. President Chun Doo-hwan, who had seized power in a military coup d'état after the assassination of President Park Chun-hee in 1979, declared martial law in May 1980. The purpose was to suppress the movement for democracy that was spreading throughout the nation. The citizens of Kwangju stood up to protest against this government action, demanding the abolition of martial law and the establishment of democracy. President Chun's response was to send in the army and crush the revolt. Some estimate the number of victims as 2,000, and the Kwangju Uprising has been recorded as the most tragic event in the history of the democratization movement in Korea. The truth was covered up by the government, and the victims were disgraced with labels of 'hoodlums', an extremely shameful accusation in Korea. Consequently, one of the crucial points in the present movement for democracy is to reveal the truth of this event so as to restore the honour of its victims. It is said that unless these wounds are healed, democracy will never be realized in South Korea.

I visited Kwangju in July 1981, the year after the uprising. This cultural city, which has produced a number of novelists and poets, was so green and peaceful I could not imagine that such a bloody massacre had taken place here just one year earlier. The life of the citizens was seemingly so calm that it was hard to believe in the hell created here. I was told that young women's breasts had been cut off, and pregnant women stabbed in the belly. The only sign of the massacre was the bullet marks on the buildings of Kumnam Street, the city's main thoroughfare.

It was taboo, however, to speak openly about that terrible event, and the citizens kept their mouths tightly closed. I myself was frightened when I entered the city, as I was conscious of trying to avoid the strict surveillance of government agents. It was dangerous even to pay tribute to the victims buried in Mangwol-Dong Cemetery in the suburbs, so I had to cancel that visit. I was told by a member of a victim's family that:

> We are not even allowed to say that my husband or my son has not come back. Some mothers still cling to the slight hope that their sons survived, and that someday they will return. This is the natural feeling of parents.

Mudung mountain is a symbol of Kwangju, the city called 'city of youth'. I visited Cho A-rah, President of Kwangju YWCA, who lives at the foot of this mountain; I also met Lee Ai-shin, YWCA general secretary there. President Cho had been detained for six months, although over seventy years old, and Lee Ai-shin for three months, following the uprising.

I met three women whose husbands were in prison. Lee Myong-ja is the wife of Chunnam University student Chung Tong-nyon who was first sentenced to death, a sentence later commuted to life imprisonment. He was charged with being the leader of the Kwangju rebellion, receiving funds from political opposition leader Kim Dae-jung, and with being a student agitator. He was so cruelly tortured that he tried in vain to commit suicide. Lee Myong-ja is struggling to make a living to support their two children.

Another woman whom I met was the wife of Myong No-gun, professor of Chunnam University. Mother of five children and head nurse at the Christian Hospital, she was a key figure in the families of political detainees. The third woman was the wife of a lawyer, Hong Nam-Sun, a man so highly respected that he was asked to be a citizen's representative in the negotiations for a solution to the stand-off between the military and the students. His wife, who had also been imprisoned, said, 'I was not allowed to sleep for nine days, but the most cruel treatment was when our third son was brought before me and my husband, and tortured before our eyes.' She covered her face as she told me this. She was released from prison, but her husband was sentenced to life imprisonment with hard labour, a sentence that was later reduced to seven years.

When I made a second visit to Kwangju in May 1985, all these political prisoners had been released and returned to their families, but the sons who were killed would never come back. I met the mothers of these sons who were killed and learned how brutally they are oppressed and how bravely they are resisting. These mothers have transformed the silent Kwangju of four years ago into an angry Kwangju.

Taking a bus south from Seoul to Kwangju, I first visited Mangwol-Dong Cemetery, high on a hill in the suburbs, and I saw about 100 black tombstones. In the twilight I listened to vivid stories from members of the Association of Families of the Kwangju 18 May Uprising Victims. Together with these family members I offered a prayer for the souls of the victims. I then visited a hospital in the city to see the mother of one victim – forty-six-year-old Kim Kil-ja. She had been about to leave her home to attend the general meeting of the Association to plan the organization of the youth section, when she was stopped by security agents who had been watching her around the clock. She was so angry that she slapped one of them; he threw his walkie-talkie at her and beat her up with a baton. Seriously injured, with a bleeding head wound, she had been taken to the hospital just three days before my visit.

Her room on the sixth floor of the hospital was crowded with mothers from the association. They expressed their anger and sorrow to me, an unexpected visitor, saying, 'We have no time for crying.' An old woman whose name was Kim Kun-dan was holding a lovely little girl on her lap.

> This is my granddaughter. When my son, her father, was killed, she was only 100 days old. He was twenty-nine. Every day I cried and cried until I nearly damaged my eyes, but now I have no more tears to shed because I am busy in activities for the democracy my son was so eager to realize. The only thing I want is to clear my son's *han*; he is still disgraced as a hoodlum.

Uniquely Korean, *han* is a deep feeling that rises out of an unjust or unwarranted experience. 'Justifiable indignation' is a common translation. Christian Ethics Professor Hyun Young-hak says, '*Han* is the suppressed, amassed, and condensed experience of oppression caused by mischief or misfortune so that it forms a kind of "lump" in one's spirit.' (*Minjung Theology*, CTC/CCA (ed.) Zed Press, London, 1983.)

On the following day, the mothers began a protest action commemorating the fifth anniversary of the Kwangju Uprising. The mothers that I had talked with at the cemetery and hospital the day before had now stationed themselves on the sixth floor of the Catholic Center. They were hanging banners from the windows and shouting through a microphone: 'Give me back my son!' 'Chun Doo-hwan resign now!', 'Don't hide the truth of the event!' A crowd of citizens gathered and the street was soon filled with policemen and their trucks. The people silently expressed their sympathy for the mothers. As I stood there among them, I could sense their feelings but, after a while, the explosions of tear gas canisters drove me away. The crowd was dispersed and all the mothers were again taken to the police station.

Having lost their beloved sons, they were afraid of nothing. Always watched by security personnel, they were taken away to remote mountain areas when VIPs came to visit the city. In spite of these precautions on the part of the government, whenever they could escape from the watchful eyes of government agents, they would shout out at visiting officials, 'Chun Doo-hwan, take responsibility!' and 'Reveal the truth of the Kwangju Uprising!' They were arrested again and again. Each time they protested they would be injured, then arrested. All those women present in the hospital room I visited had bruised bodies; they were literally sacrificing themselves to the struggle. They were motivated to achieve the end results towards which their sons had given their lives; and it was these aspirations that closely united them.

When I recall my over ten-year involvement with the Korean democratization movement, it is the power of mothers and other women that impresses me more deeply than anything else. Chung Kum-song, mother of resistance poet Kim Chi-ha, who has been imprisoned many times, played an important role as the co-ordinator of leaders of the movement who were on the list of persons wanted by government security agents. In spite of the tight watch by the Korean Central Intelligence Agency (KCIA) and the danger of arrest, she always encouraged the families of political detainees. She was proud of her son Kim Chi-ha, and when he was under sentence of death, she said, 'I want to support him so that he can keep his belief until the last moment.'

Kang Sun-hi, wife of one of the eight falsely accused victims of execution mentioned above, wrote a poem of lament when her husband was taken away. 'Probably we anticipated our destiny of such a sad separation. That's why we loved each other so deeply.' Her advice to her young children was, 'Your father is innocent. Please live with pride in him.' And she pledged that she herself would live with courage, 'because I believe the day will surely come when the *han* embedded in the heart of the nation will be resolved'. I was deeply touched by her expressions of sadness.

It is, in fact, the Japanese now in power who support the government of South Korea; it is this government that has pushed this mother, and many others, into the depths of despair. Therefore, the only way for me to become her friend is to challenge the power structure of Japan. Thus, we must think about the relationship between Korean women who are struggling for national liberation and democracy and we Japanese women.

I heard of a prayer offered by a mother whose two sons were in prison: 'Please forgive my sin that I prayed to You only for the release of my own children. We should love other people's children just as much as we do our own.' This is a beautiful concept of a broader and more noble maternal love, an example of unselfish love. One mother whom I met in Kwangju commented: 'Now those who are ugly and those who are beautiful are fighting. I must do my best to endure this pain so that the victory of the beautiful ones can be realized.'

South Korea has been developing its economy by using the threat of invasion from the North to control the anti-establishment forces that are struggling for democracy; and the gap between the rich and the poor is widening. Under these conditions, 'those who are beautiful', or those people of the democratization movement, have had to make immeasurable sacrifices. Even so, their struggle is continuing. *Han*, the 'justifiable indignation' of the mothers who lost their sons, has become the driving force that supports this struggle.

11.
Women Forging a Future:
Emerging Asian Feminist Movements

Introduction

New feminist movements are emerging in Asian countries. Since the 1980s, women's organizations one after another have been formed in each country. They all have two objectives: liberation from political and economic oppression and, at the same time, liberation from sexual discrimination based on patriarchy. In other words, national liberation movements and social structural changes are combined with women's liberation.

To establish linkage among these feminist organizations, the Asian Women's Research and Action Network (AWRAN) organized an Asian Women's Conference in Davao City, in the southern part of Mindanao Island in the Philippines, in spring 1985. I had the opportunity to participate in this conference with delegates from fourteen Asian countries, all of whom were women activists in feminist groups in their respective countries. Because they shared so many common experiences it took very little time for these women from different cultures, different political and economic systems, and different lifestyles, concerned with different issues, to become close friends and share feelings of sisterhood. Sexual discrimination, and the struggle to overcome it, was common to them all, as were their aspirations for a new society, free from all oppression. Irene Santiago, an AWRAN organizer from the Philippines, expressed the aspirations of these women's groups:

> We are bound as victims of political, economic, social, and cultural structures in Asian realities, and these are very strong ties. But stronger still are the ties that bind us as lovers of justice, peace, equality, and life for, in the end, that is what we are working for; that all may live truly human lives as women and men.

What kind of feminist movements are growing in each country?

The Philippines

In the host country, the Philippines, the women's movement, GABRIELA, was founded in 1984. This is a coalition of more than seventy groups of women from various walks of life, such as workers and rural women, and those concerned with issues such as prostitution, migration and human rights. The name itself comes from Gabriela Silan, heroine in Philippine history who replaced her slain husband as a leader in the revolutionary army against Spanish rule in the eighteenth century, and who was executed. GABRIELA is playing an important role in setting the direction of both national and women's liberation.

Under the Marcos dictatorship, a people's movement had been growing but, until the early 1980s, the feminist movement was coldly looked upon as an imitation of the women's liberation movement in the West. The objective of the Philippine women's movement was to mobilize as many women as possible for the national liberation struggle, and to fight together with men for economic rights, political democracy, independence from foreign domination, and many other kinds of social justice.

To illustrate this, in autumn 1981 at a study seminar on women workers in South-east Asia in Colombo, Sri Lanka, Philippine human rights activist Edith Tores spoke strongly: 'We women in the Philippines are very busy in the struggle against dictatorship. Therefore, a separate movement of only women may be detrimental to the struggle for change in social structure.' When, however, she attended the 1983 Bombay conference, Asian Women in Struggle for Justice, she turned out to be a militant feminist. This is probably because issues that Filipino women have to face – prostitution tourism, overseas migration as domestic workers and mail-order brides, rape and sexual torture – were becoming more and more serious because of the deterioration of the economic situation. In response to this, all kinds of small women's groups sprang up to deal with specific issues: for example, Third World Women Against Exploitation; STOP; Women's Center; Filipina. They were influenced by the United Nations Women's Decade, and also stimulated by the expanding feminist movement in the Third World.

The feminist force in the Philippines represented by GABRIELA grew to be the most advanced movement in both theory and in practice. The country report submitted to the Davao conference was the collective work of sixteen women. It began with an analysis of the situation of Asian women who suffer from the three-fold oppression of nationality, class, and gender: as Third World people, they are oppressed by foreign dominance; as the working class, by their own ruling elite; and as women, by male domination based on patriarchy. The report clearly defines the strategy of a women's movement for liberation from such oppression as requiring three principles: it must be rooted in the people, based on feminism, and inseparable from national liberation and class struggle. With such a well-thought-out and clearly articulated self-understanding, the women's movement in the Philippines was becoming more and more powerful; it was challenging the system by organizing such struggles as women workers' strikes, campaigns against sex tourism, and anti-Marcos movements.

Originally, the Philippines had a unique culture that gave high status to women. Agricultural production and domestic work was shared by both men and women. In some tribes the performance of religious functions was in the hands of women and women were given political power. Colonization by Spain in the sixteenth century led to the ideal image of women as Virgin Mary types in the Catholic Church and to the introduction of European-type patriarchy. As a result, women became downgraded and subjugated to men. Later, as a colony of the United States, a limited degree of equality between men and women was tolerated. Establishment-oriented women's organizations were formed by elitist women for the purpose of charity work, and these groups continue to function. Towards the end of the 1960s, amid the growing national liberation struggle and student movement, the first feminist organization MAKIBAKA was formed. Soon after this, martial law was declared and MAKIBAKA's leader, Lorena Barros, went underground; she was shot by government troops in 1976. Thus, the feminist movement was nipped in the bud, but the resolution was revived almost ten years later in GABRIELA.

In explaining their purpose GABRIELA says:

> Women stepped out of the traditional roles assigned to them to participate in the political struggle in a broader and deeper way. They also began to take action to get rid of discrimination against women in any form. These were the objectives in forming this coalition.

On International Woman's Day, 8 March 1986, the rally organized by GABRIELA in Luneta Park in Manila was a huge success (see Chapter 9). In the heat of the collapse of the Marcos regime and the rise of the Aquino government, the long-oppressed women's power exploded in a celebration of victory. Having gained more confidence under a woman President, the Filipino women are a great encouragement to other Asian women.

Pakistan

Nighat Said Khan was also a powerful symbol for women in the struggle against the Islamization policy in her country. She reported to the Davao conference: 'In Pakistan under the present military regime, women are taking the lead for social change, and the women's issue is now a national issue.' In this country, where the illiteracy rate for women is as high as eighty-four percent, grass-roots women are not yet mobilized as they are in the Philippines. But, since autumn 1981, educated women who felt threatened by the intensifying discrimination against women in the Islamization policy formed the Women's Action Forum (WAF) in Karachi, Lahore, Islamabad, Peshawar, and other cities. Actions such as street demonstrations have been organized (see Chapter 7).

In February 1982, the Lahore WAF held a rally and demonstration against the discriminatory Law of Evidence that states: 'In a court case, two women are necessary to give witness but only one man is required.' About 300 women participated in this demonstration; more than twenty were wounded and thirty-one arrested. This was the first demonstration after the military regime took power in 1977. It gave an impression to the whole nation that 'the most powerful and persistent opposition force against the martial law regime is women', and it became the forerunner of the movement for democracy, which has expanded since 1983.

I met women of the WAF for the first time when I visited the old city of Lahore in autumn 1983. In a backyard corner of a house in the residential district, thirty or forty women in colourful Punjabi dress (long tunic over loose pants) were making placards in secret. 'We are against the law of evidence that treats women as half persons', and 'Stop the barbarous punishment of whipping', were messages written in beautiful flowing Urdu script. Then, a woman arrived a little late and all the women jumped up to greet her saying, 'Congratulations on your release', 'Were you beaten up?'; 'Are you all right?' Lovingly and warmly, they took her hands and embraced her. 'Look, I'm quite all right,' she said with a smile. This slender housewife, Faryal Gauhal, had been arrested just ten days before during a demonstration against martial law and demands for democracy. Twelve women had been arrested, including some with children, pregnant women, and one old woman of over seventy years. Faryal said, 'The military regime under the Islamization policy has pushed women's status backwards into the medieval dark age. In order to stop this, we need democracy. That's why I participated in this demonstration.' She did not seem tired after ten days' detention and promptly started to help make the placards.

Shortly afterwards, walking in twos and threes and carrying the newly-made placards concealed from view, the women headed toward the state governor's residence. Their thin veils were not on their heads in the traditional way, but resting on their shoulders, and they moved with light steps. Arriving at the front gate, they stood in a row and hoisted their placards and banners high in front of their faces. Within less than fifteen minutes, a police car arrived and a megaphone was used to order the women to disperse. Then, a grim-faced policeman armed with a rifle approached the line of women. They did not shrink but appealed to the police, 'This is the problem of your mother, your wife, and your daughters. Do you accept the fact that they are not treated as human beings because they are women?' The bearded police leader, smiling sourly, shouted, 'Disperse, disperse.' The women had agreed beforehand that this time no one should be arrested, so they left after about thirty minutes. The WAF members repeatedly demonstrate, sometimes prepared for arrest and sometimes quite peacefully, to protest against the Islamization policy.

Even though this movement is led by mainly urban intellectual women, their concern extends to all Pakistan's women. One said:

It is the poor women who are victimized most cruelly by bad laws of discrimination against women. Because we have connections, class and family for example, we are not whipped under adultery laws. This is why we have an obligation to speak up and fight for the women who are struggling just to survive from one day to the next.

After their demonstration outside the governor's residence, members of the WAF were again made aware of the need for their chosen role when they read in their morning newspaper:

A thirty-five-year-old widow, charged with adultery, was subjected to the punishment of whipping before a crowd of more than 5,000. She was allowed to remain veiled and was carried to the hospital screaming with pain.

I flew from Lahore to Karachi and here, too, WAF was very active.

One of its members is a reporter on a leading daily newspaper that gives wide coverage to women's issues. I attended a rally, 'Women and Democracy', organized by WAF. This was a heated meeting attended by more than 200 women. One after another, delegates from various sectors of society spoke out: 'Both men and women are deprived of democratic political rights. Let women and men fight against military dictatorship side by side.' 'No political movement can be successful without the participation of women.' 'Unless we restore democracy, we cannot carry on the struggle for women's liberation.' In Lahore and in Karachi, it became clear to me that the political struggle and the feminist struggle cannot be separated in Third World countries.

Nighat expressed the women's aspirations succinctly, saying that:

> We feminists are condemned because we are trying to challenge all forms of patriarchy, and to change society radically, not just achieve legal and economic reform within the system. We want to be free from all kinds of oppression. We search for power to control our own lives and bodies, for internal strength.

Truly, women must have great courage if they want to speak up in Islamic society. Feminist movements such as WAF are abused and slandered with stereotypical labels such as 'Westernized', or 'elitist', 'fractional activities', and so forth, by progressives as well as conservatives.

Linkage with grass-roots women, steady day-to-day movement activities in combination with political struggle, a vision for the twenty-first century, are all characteristics of the feminist movement in this country. It was a great surprise to me that such a well-organized feminist movement could emerge in this Islamic country which, at that time, was under a politically repressive military government; and also enduring the cultural oppression of religious traditions and sexual discrimination. I was convinced that nothing could stop this movement for liberation and advancement.

South Korea

Those countries with a Confucian cultural tradition are also feeling the impact of such movements. Cho Hyoung, delegate from South Korea at the Davao conference, is a young professor of sociology at Ewha Women's University, and one of the founders of Women for Equality and Peace (see Chapter 10). Founded in 1983 by some thirty women intellectuals, including doctors, teachers, and journalists, they have raised funds of ten million *won* (about 2.2 million yen). 'More than anything else, we put emphasis on activities to support women workers, slum mothers, and other poor women.' Cho Hyoung stressed that their organization aimed at a grass-roots oriented movement; a very active women's labour movement in the 1970s is part of its historical background.

In South Korea, under an export-oriented rapid economic development policy, women are exploited as cheap labour, and their human rights are violated without compunction. Despite this, courageous struggles are continually organized. A Christian woman pastor, Cho Wha-sun, began work as a factory hand in the Inchon Tong-il Textile Company for the purpose of consciousness-raising among women workers. And, in 1972, a woman was elected for the first time as the chairperson of the trade union branch. This union was transformed into a democratic organ that protected the rights of its women workers and, for this reason, was brutally suppressed by government authorities and harassed by 'yellow' (pro-government) unions. The women workers resisted with hunger strikes and sit-ins; they were beaten up, arrested, or dismissed. In an infamous incident in 1978, the women protesters were smeared with human faeces and urine by company-hired thugs, and Pastor Cho was imprisoned. The poor women workers of Tong-il Textile Company never yielded, and continued with their demand, 'We just want to live as human beings.'

A famous anti-government nationalist poet, Ko-un, wrote:

My dear daughters,
You are leaders to guide our nation.
I want to follow you,
Ashamed,
With all my strength,
Exploding burning righteous resentment.
I'm determined to follow your path.

The struggle at the Tong-il Textile factory, together with Lee So-sun's brave fight at Seoul's Peace Market (see Chapter 10) will be recorded as historical events. In the 1980s it was the women who led the labour movement in South Korea, under incredible suppression.

Historically speaking, South Korea still has a strong ideology of sexual discrimination influenced by Confucian culture, and women are considered as the property of men. A woman had a family name but not a personal one and, after marriage, she continued to be known by this family name because her in-laws did not recognize her as a full member of their family and therefore she was not permitted to use her husband's name. As in Japanese and Chinese feudal societies, women were never treated as human beings. Then, in 1910, Korea was colonized by Japan for 36 years, and women's plight deteriorated even further. In spite of such circumstances, a number of women stood in the front lines in the national liberation struggles.

A symbol of this resistance was Yu Kwan-sun, a sixteen-year-old woman known as the 'Joan of Arc of Korea'. During the March First Independence Movement uprising in 1919, she carried the banned Korean flag and encouraged her compatriots to resist with the rallying cry, 'Let's shout "long live independence".' During the demonstration, her parents were shot dead and she was arrested. At her trial, she fearlessly insisted, 'It is the Japanese who are criminals. Those Japanese have no right to judge us.' In prison, she continued her struggle claiming, 'While I am alive, long live independence. Even after I die, long live independence.' She was brutally tortured and her body was covered with scars; she finally died in prison in 1920.

In this rebellion, on 1 March 1919, against the harsh colonization policies of the Japanese, the energies of women all over the country, from schoolgirls to *kisaeng* (professional hostesses, entertainers, and sometimes prostitutes) exploded in participation. This courageous spirit, evident in the national anti-Japanese struggle, was carried over after World War Two liberation into the democratization movement and the labour movement. But the women's movement itself, even though the numbers of groups increased to almost 100, remained under the leadership of women who had been pro-Japanese during the colonial period, and who continued to support the dictatorial regime that followed World War Two. Moreover, as the economy was developing, the women's movement was led by economically better-off middle-class housewives, and little attention was paid to the urgent issues of poor working women.

Toward the end of the 1960s, author Choe Ok-ja's biting criticisms in her thesis, 'Reflections on the Women's Movement', were directed to those women leaders who offered thousands and thousands of Korean women to the Japanese army as prostitutes, and who had continued as leaders up to that time.

In the 1970s, the rapid economic growth known as the 'miracle of the Han River' was promoted by exploiting women as cheap labour, based on their sex role as determined by Confucian patriarchy. As a result, the gap between the rich and the poor widened, and women workers resisted by organizing a militant labour movement. Thus, criticism against establishment-oriented women's movements, the struggle of women workers, and the influence of the United Nations Women's Decade, all came together in complementary interaction and paved the way for the new feminist movement of the 1980s.

Women for equality and peace

South Korea's major feminist group in the 1980s is Women for Equality and Peace, challenging a patriarchy that victimizes women, as well as the government's economic growth policy. According to this organization's first publication in 1983, its objectives and principles are: firstly, to work out a theory of women's issues in the Korean situation; secondly, to co-operate with other social movements to build a new society in which women can live as human beings; thirdly, it should be a mass movement in the interests of the poorest, the most oppressed, and the most alienated women; and fourthly, it should have a democratic management that allows individual members to participate and to act. The organization emphasizes that:

> Unless women are liberated, human liberation is impossible. Unless a society where women can live as human beings is realized, women's liberation will remain only an illusion. Women's liberation is an inseparable part of the society of liberated human beings.

The sponsorship of the slum project in Inchon (Chapter 10) and organizing a women's cultural festival for women workers are based on these ideals. The 1985 festival was an attempt to raise consciousness about women's conditions by using songs, dances, and drama. Different from other women's organizations, this group has a fresh sense of what young women find appealing, and some 2,000 women workers rushed to the festival hall. The same performance had to be presented four times to satisfy the demand.

This organization was also busy in efforts to pinpoint specific issues of discrimination against women. For example, they protested against the maternity retirement system; they criticized the amount of compensation for female traffic accident victims as being much lower than for male victims; they condemned the sexual torture of a woman student by the police. Using these incidents, they appealed to public opinion.

The external factor that constrains the organized movement of women is politics. If a woman's organization takes an anti-government position, it will face very strict regulations or outright suppression. So far already, not the organization itself, but several individual members have been subject to such harassment, and the group itself is under severe surveillance.

The speaker was quite frank about the difficulty of feminist movements under an oppressive political system that is common to Third World countries. She went on, 'Even so, for the first time in our country women's issues are broadly and seriously taken up.' She also emphasized that women's power could no longer be neglected.

Taiwan and Hong Kong

Nora Lan Hung Chiang, an assistant professor in the geography department of Taiwan National University, was also a participant in the Davao conference. Like South Korea, Taiwan is a Confucian society under long-time martial law. 'The Chinese Nationalist government gives top priority to political stability and anti-communist ideology. For that purpose, it has imposed on women the Chinese traditional concept of "a woman's place is in the home". Our biggest task,' she said, 'is to break through it.'

Lu Hsui-Lien had studied law at Harvard University in the United States. She also wanted to change such traditional sex roles and in 1972 initiated a feminist movement that advocated a 'new womanism'. She began a 'telephone to protect you' service for women in order to help poor women and victims of violence; she also launched a campaign to liberalize abortion. Not only a strong feminist, but also a strong nationalist, participating in the Taiwan Independence and Democracy Movement, she became a militant fighter for feminism and national liberation. Arrested in 1979, she was charged with involvement in the Kaohsiung Incident where about 30,000 citizens demanding democracy at a Human Rights Day rally collided with police force. Lu Hsui-Lien was imprisoned with a twelve-year sentence and the feminist movement was crushed – it became taboo.

Nevertheless, in 1982, women in Taipei formed a group and began to publish a newsletter, *Awakening*, for the purpose of consciousness-raising. Also, due to the influence of the United Nations Women's Decade, in 1984, the Eugenics Production Law was amended to liberalize abortion. This had been a target of women's struggle since Lu Hsui-Lien's advocacy fifteen years before.

'The feminist movement is quiet compared with the consumers

movement or the environmental movement, because under the present political situation, the government does not welcome any new social movements, and the new women's movement is not an exception,' said Lan Hung Chiang. Compared with Pakistan or South Korea where the women are struggling in spite of severe oppression, people's movements or anti-establishment movements are still tightly controlled in Taiwan. Lu Hsui-Lien's imprisonment is a case in point; 'New Womanism' was effectively crushed because she remained isolated from her potential support.

In Hong Kong, a Confucian society, and also a British colony, there was no feminist movement, even after the beginning of the United Nations Decade for Women. Then, in 1984, a group of young women organized the Society for the Advancement of Women's Status, the first of its kind in Hong Kong. They are trying to change women's consciousness by means of drama and so forth '. . . to take action from a grass-roots women's level, and change the role of women in society'.

South-east Asia

Most women's groups in South-east Asian countries take up specific issues. In Thailand, the feminist group organized in 1980, Women's Friends, confronts one of the most serious problems in that country – prostitution. In January 1981, when former Japanese Prime Minister Zenko Suzuki visited Bangkok on his tour of ASEAN countries, these women handed a letter to the Japanese Embassy condemning prostitution tourism; they also performed a street drama nearby to appeal to the public on this issue.

Later on, Siriporn Skrobanek began a Women's Information Center to counsel women who are planning to go abroad to work in the sex industry. This centre has recently opened up a shelter for battered women. Also, in 1985, Chantawipa Apisuk organized the group Empower and started classes in English to help prostitutes to become self-reliant (Chapter 5). All of these Thai women's groups are trying to strengthen and extend the movements that work against the perception of women as commodities, and the violence visited on them.

In Malaysia, the Women's Aid Organization (WAO) was formed in 1982, and a shelter was opened in a private house in a suburb of Kuala Lumpur, the capital city; women who suffer violence at the hands of their husbands can take refuge there. This shelter is staffed by volunteers and when I visited in 1984, one of them said to me:

> The causes of violence are varied, and can differ slightly according to the ethnic group. For example, Indian women face poverty and alcoholism; Malay, love affairs; Chinese, money problems are common. However, husbands who beat their wives can belong to any profession and come from any class, although the women who come to this shelter are mostly poor women, as rich women have other alternatives. Here, women of different ethnic groups, mothers in similar circumstances, encourage each other, heal their wounded feelings, and recover confidence to start their lives again.

This shelter reflects the plural society of Malaysia, and helps those women who have given up and simply endured their husbands' violence to stand up and protect themselves.

In autumn 1984, WAO and four other women's groups formed a Coalition Opposing Violence Against Women, and held their first rally in Kuala Lumpur in spring 1985, to protest against rape, prostitution, and many other such violent acts committed against women. 'The feminist movement in Asia is quite new and this rally is only a first step. I expect this movement to respond to the problems of poor women,' said Anizan Isahak, lecturer at the University of Malaya, in a rather low-key speech at the Davao conference. In this country also, the women's movement experiences very serious restrictions such as government control under the Internal Security Act, and ethnic polarization.

Singapore, an island state in the southern part of the Malay Peninsula, is under an even stricter political system. The independent organization of any non-government movement is totally banned. In the summer of 1984, Prime Minister Lee Kuan Yew said, 'If poor mothers without education have many children, it will endanger the future of our state. Highly educated women should have more brilliant children.' His selective family planning policy is based on his own eugenic ideology and IQ (intelligence quotient) priority theory. His decision was to give privileges to the enrolment of children of university graduate mothers in the nation's schools. Many women have criticized this as an 'elitist population policy', but an openly organized opposition is out of the question.

This mini-state, a former British colony whose population during that time mainly comprised poor Chinese immigrants, has achieved outstanding economic development since the 1970s, and has raised the educational standards for its women. Consequently, it could no longer escape the tidal wave of women's liberation movements. Consequently, in spring 1986, the first feminist organization, Asian Women's Action Research (AWARE), was formed by researchers, writers, and other intellectual women. 'We have to start by studying what kinds of sexual discrimination we are to deal with.' These action-oriented members had made a rather cautious start. At each monthly meeting, more than 100 young women participated and discussed such things as sexual harassment and discrimination in the office environment. But no matter how small the start of this organization for women's self-reliance, it is an epoch-making event in a country under such tight political control.

Indonesia, a big power situated even farther south, has a huge population of more than 115 million, and involvement in politics is restricted for women in this country, too. Even though it has an impressive history of women activists, such as Ms. Kartini, the first advocate of national liberation under Dutch colonial rule, and KOWANI, Women's Congress of Indonesia, which played an important role in the independence movement, today, under the present dictatorial regime, it is extremely difficult to organize an independent feminist movement. Furthermore, tight government control that reaches even the grass-roots forces many women to join Darma Wanita and other government-sponsored women's organizations, according to the gloomy report from an Indonesian participant at the Davao conference.

Indonesia does, however, retain a matriarchal tradition that pre-dates the advent of Islam, and differs from Pakistan and Middle Eastern Islamic countries in that Indonesian women participate in production labour and very many are active in public life. In spite of having abundant natural resources, Indonesia is the least economically developed country in all of South-east Asia and, for the majority of its women, the most urgent issue is liberation from sheer poverty.

India

In contrast to Indonesia India enjoys a degree of political freedom that is exceptional in Asia. Numerous women's liberation groups are being organized throughout the entire country, dealing with a variety of issues such as rape, dowry, child marriage, prostitution, slum women, landless peasant women, minority women, and so on (see Chapter 6).

They take action in co-operation with each other, and during the United Nations Women's Decade old-established women's organizations were reactivated and new groups formed.

Indian women are vocal at any women's conference, and Vibbhuti Patel, who had left her newborn baby at home when she attended the Davao conference, is no exception and full of energy.

> During the past decade, violence against women has been growing, but the struggle to challenge this has been strengthened. New kinds of women's groups that are not affiliated to any political party or religious group have emerged, and at least this decade of women's movement has forced all political parties to be more alert to women's problems. They can no longer ignore this as a Western import. While the necessity to theorize about the root causes of discrimination against women is recognized, confrontational violent actions are also being taken.

After introducing the struggles taking place in various areas, she concluded:

> More and more women are aware that unless women themselves struggle, no discrimination or oppression will be wiped out. How to stir up a mass movement, a mobilization of the grass-roots women who are struggling day after day against poverty – this is our task from now on.

Sri Lanka

As one of the founders of the Asian Women's Research and Action Network (AWRAN), Hema Goonatilake of Sri Lanka, a lecturer at Kelaniya University, gave a keynote report at the Davao conference. She is a quiet and gentle person, but once she speaks out, her words are tough and militant. An attractive woman as are many Asian feminist activists, she has published a comprehensive report on Sri Lankan women, a joint effort with six other women.

> Sri Lankan women suffer between two roles: they benefit from and are also victims of this country's development policy. The United Nations Women's Decade made them visible but the reality of where they are placed has not changed. Furthermore, under the present government's open economic policy, Sri Lanka is more

economically dependent on the advanced countries, and the situation of its women has been deteriorating.

This analysis, exposing a problem common to Third World countries from a global perspective, was very convincing.

Hema spoke about the new women's movement in Sri Lanka that was organized under such difficult circumstances:

> Our struggle cannot be fulfilled only by men and women achieving equality in an unequal society. We are struggling for a radical change of such a society, and for the principle of participation in it, and the self-reliance of poor women.

Voice of Women, a group formed in Sri Lanka in 1978, is Asia's first feminist women's group, and its strategy is based on the above-mentioned principles. Members of this group, whom I met at the 1981 seminar on women workers in Colombo, were dealing with problems of women workers in rural villages, on plantations, in export processing zones, migrant women in the Middle East, violence against women, images of women in the media, and many other issues faced by Sri Lankan women. But they also realize that, 'As long as women in one country are slaves, men of that country can never be free.' As Hema said in her conclusion, 'The struggle of women for change cannot be isolated from the struggle of the poor and the oppressed in any society. Women's struggle should be linked to the common struggle against oppression in all forms.'

Summing up, the Asian feminist movement maintains its own identity while co-operating with various people's movements, and aims to build an oppression-free society. The future of Asia will be opened up by these women who join hands to step forward from the pits of poverty, oppression, and despair. Women's Asia is quietly burning.

Postscript:
Thanks to All Asian Women

'The Japanese coming to other Asian countries were military men in the past. Today, they are businessmen and tourists. Why don't they come as our friends?' This question was posed to me on my arrival in Singapore as *Asahi Shimbun*'s Asia Correspondent. In answering, I had to admit that having been a military power in the region, Japan is now an economic power, and that very few Japanese question this role for their country. Also, few Japanese try to share or are even aware of the suffering of other Asians, or try to live together with them as good neighbours.

This difficult question came from Lai Ah Eng, a Chinese–Malaysian who was my housemate for three and a half years in Singapore. Her mother's first husband was an anti-Japanese guerrilla during World War Two, and was killed by Japanese troops at Hainan Island, just off the south coast of the Chinese mainland. In spite of such bitter experiences in her family, she treated me – a Japanese – warmly, and I was greatly encouraged by her friendship.

Without the help of many such women in each of the Asian countries that I visited, I could not have made these journeys by myself. Now, when I recall their faces, one by one, I feel that the only way to express my gratitude for their warmth and kindness is to encourage as many Japanese as possible to treat other Asian peoples as true friends. It is with such a wish that I have written this book.

Sawako Tabata of the Iwanami Publishing Company suggested that I write it some three years ago during my stay in Singapore. After my return to Japan, I was too busy as a reporter, but she continued to encourage, and to scold me. Without her support I could not have conveyed to the readers the compelling voices of Asian women in this form.

From the bottom of my heart, I express my thanks to countless friends in Japan and in other Asian countries.

Yayori Matsui
February 1987

Sources

Chapter 1

Activity Report, Shapla News, Dhaka: Shapla Neer (1983).

Arthur, W. B., & G. McNicoll, 'An Analytical Survey on Population and Development in Bangladesh'. *Population and Development Review* (1978).

Asian Action, *Newsletter of the Asian Cultural Forum on Development.* Bangkok (1983).

AWAKE *Asian Women and the Struggle for Justice.* Sydney, Asia Partnership for Human Development (1985).

Bangladesh Institute of Law & International Affairs, Report of Legal Aspects of Population Planning in Bangladesh (1978).

Bangladesh & UNFPA, *Background Paper on Annual Country Review.* Dhaka Government of Bangladesh (1981).

Beguml, Mosammat Sufia, *A Field Worker Experience.* Bangladesh, n.p. (1979).

Chaudhury, Rifiqul Huda, *Urbanization in Bangladesh.* Dacca, n.p. (1980).

Khanum, Sultana, 'Infection Pattern of Malnourished Children in Children's Unit'. Dacca: Medical Director, Children's Unit, n.d.

Malakar, Mina, Christian Health Center Project. *Workshop Minutes for Rural Women Workers.* Barisal, Bangladesh, n.p. (1982).

Matsui, Yayori, 'My Visit to Red Light Districts in Asia'. *Chuokoronsha* (1985).

Ratcliffe, J. W., *Poverty, Politics and Fertility: The Anomaly of Kerala.* India, Hastings Center Report (1977).

'The Situation of Women in Bangladesh'. Dacca, Women for Women (1979).

UNICEF, 'Statistical Profile of Children and Mothers in Bangladesh'. Bangladesh (1979).

Chapter 2

Commission on Theological Concerns, *For the Dawning of the New.* Singapore, Christian Conference of Asia (1981).

Dawood, Nawaz, *Tea and Poverty: Plantations and the Political Economy of Sri Lanka.* Hong Kong, Urban Rural Mission, Christian Conference of Asia (1980).

'The Exploitation of Women in the Plantation Sector'. *Voice of Women, A Sri Lanka Journal for Women's Emancipation* (1980).

Heyzer, Noeleen, *Working Women in Southeast Asia; Development, Subordination and Emancipation*. Philadelphia, Open University Press (1986).

Jayawardena, Kumari, 'Exploitation of Women in Plantations – Tamil Women Workers in Tea Plantations'. Colombo, Sri Lanka, Women's Education Center (1986).

Jeyakumar, D., 'The Indian Poor in Malaysia: Problems and Solutions'. Paper presented at international conference on Modernization and National Identity organized by Malaysian Social Science Association, Kuala Lumpur, Malaysia (1983).

Jomo, K. S., 'Early Labour: Children at Work on Malaysian Plantations'. Kuala Lumpur, Malaysia Institute for Social Analysis (1984).

Lai, Ah Eng, *Peasants, Proletarians and Prostitutes: A Preliminary Investigation into the Work of Chinese Women in Colonial Malaya*. Singapore, Institute of Southeast Asian Studies (1986).

Magno, Linda S., 'Harvest for a Few Profits and Poverty in the Mindanao Export Fruits Industry'. *Showcases of Underdevelopment*. Philippines, n.p. (1984).

Meena: A Plantation Child Worker from Malaysia. Petaling Jaya, Malaysia, Institute for Social Analysis (1985).

'WSRC Begins Research on Plantation Workers'. *Womenews* (1985).

Chapter 3

Anthony, Rita, 'Experiences in Organising Women Workers in Malaysia'. Malaysia, n.p. (n.d).

Ariffin, Jamilah, 'Women Workers in the Manufacturing Industries', from *Malaysian Women*. Consumers Association of Penang, Penang, Malaysia (1983).

Asian Women Workers, *Newsletter*, quarterly, Hong Kong. n.d.

Castro, Judy S., *The Bataan Export Processing Zone*. ILO-ARTEP, Bangkok, Thailand. n.d.

Daud, Fatimah, 'Women in Industry' from *Ilmu Masayarakat*, Malaysian Social Science Association Publication, Kuala Lumpur, Malaysia (1982).

'Export Processing Zones in Developing Countries'. UNIDO Working Papers on Structural Changes, New York, USA (1980).

Heyzer, Noeleen, *Working Women in Southeast Asia: Women and the Relocation of the Textile Industry*. Philadelphia, Open University Press (1986).

Neumann, A. Lin, 'Philippines Workers Strike, Triumph at Export Processing Zone'. Manila, Philippines (1982).

Smith, Wendy, A., 'The Impact of Japanese Foreign Investment and Management Style on Female Industrial Workers in Malaysia'. A paper presented at the Conference on Women in the Urban and Industrial Workforce: Southeast and East Asia. Manila, Philippines (1982).

—— 'Japanese Factory: Malaysian Workers' from *The Sun Also Sets*. INSAN, Malaysia (1983).

—— 'Industrial Relations in Japanese Large Enterprises – a Critique of the "Japanese Management" Model', a paper presented at a Seminar in Kuala Lumpur, Malaysia (1984).

Tse, Christina, *Reflections on Japanese Management: Letters to a Woman Worker*. Center for the Progress of Peoples, Hong Kong (1982).

'Women in the Redeployment of Manufacturing Industry to Developing Countries'. UNIDO Working Papers on Structural Changes. New York, USA (1980).
Workers Situation and Problems in Mariveles, compiled by Thomson, A. Mariveles, Philippines: n.p. (1981).

Chapter 4

Aquino, Lea, 'Preliminary Situation and Analysis of Filipino Labour Outmigration'. Paper presented at the CCA Conference on Migration. Manila, Philippines (1984).
Barnard, P. & Chew, L., 'Centre to Fight Maid "Abuse"', from the *Sunday Times*, Singapore (1984).
Claire, R. & Cottingham, J., 'Migration and Tourism: An Overview', from *Migration Today*, World Council of Churches. Geneva, Switzerland (n.d).
Filipino Workers: Off to Distant Shores. Mission for Filipino Migrant Workers, Hong Kong (1983).
Latif Nargis, 'The Grass is not Always Greener on the Other Side' and other newspaper articles. Karachi, Pakistan (1983).
Migrant Labour For Sale? Documentation for Action Groups in Asia (DAGA) CCA-URM, Kowloon, Hong Kong (1986)
'Migrant Women Claim Their Rights: Nairobi and After'. World Council of Churches, Geneva, Switzerland (1986).
Migration from the Philippines, compiled by Paganoni, A., Scalabrinians, Manila, Philippines (1984).
Migration Today (monthly). World Council of Churches, Geneva, Switzerland.
'Strangers Within Our Gates'. A report on Asian Women's Migration. Christian Conference of Asia, Singapore (n.d).
Vajarasathien, Chitrnath, 'A Poem Devoted to Thai Workers in Saudi Arabia', from *Migrant Labour For Sale*. DAGA, CCA-URM, Hong Kong (1986).

Chapter 5

Ekachai, Sanitsuda, 'The Dark Society: Growing Tragedy of the Brothel Children: A Special Report'. *Bangkok Post*, Thailand (1984).
―――― 'Patpong bar girls get their own newspaper', *Bangkok Post*, Thailand (1986).
'The Export of Filipino Entertainers'. *Philippine Migration Review* (quarterly newsletter of KAIBIGAN) Manila, Philippines (1987).
'Ground Down by the Japanese Sex Machine' from *Solidaridad II*, Resource Center on Philippine Concerns. Tokyo, Japan (1980).
Hantrakul, Sukanya, 'Prostitution in Thailand'. Paper presented at the Women in Asia Workshop, Monash University, Melbourne, Australia (1983).
Matsui, Y. & Park, S. A., 'Theological Reflections on the Prostitution Industry', CTC Bulletin. CCA, Singapore (1983).
Moselina, Leopoldo M., 'Olangapo's Rest & Recreation Industry: A

Sociological Analysis of Institutionalized Prostitution – With Implications for a Grassroots-Oriented Sociology'. Asian Social Institute, Philippines (1979).

O'Grady, Ron, *Third World Stopover: The Tourism Debate*. World Council of Churches, Geneva, Switzerland (1981).

'Olongapo's R & R Industry'. Makataq, Asian Social Institute, Philippines (1981).

Promporn, 'Is There a Tomorrow for Child Prostitutes?' *Bangkok Post*, Thailand (1984).

'Sex Tourism and Military Occupation', *Asian Women's Liberation*, No. 6, occasional publication of the Asian Women's Association, Tokyo, Japan (1984).

'The Situation of Young Women in the Service and Entertainment Industries in the ESCAP Region'. ESCAP, Bangkok, Thailand (1985).

Skrobanek, Siriporn, 'Three Women' from *Beyond Stereotypes: Asian Women in Development. Southeast Asia Chronicle*, Berkeley, USA (1985).

Soriano, Marcelo B., 'Prostitutes, 8 to 14, Hospitalized for VD' and others. Olongapo, Philippines (1982).

Srisang, Koson, 'Tourism Promotion and its Effects on Thai Women'. Seminar paper, Bangkok, Thailand (1986).

Third World Tourism, a report of a Workshop on Tourism, Manila, Philippines, CCA, Singapore (1980).

Tono, Haruhi, 'Why Does Japan Need Asian Women Migrant Workers?' from *Women's Link*, occasional publication of CCA–Women (1986).

Why Must We Suffer? Asian Migrant Workers, DAGA, CCA-URM, Hong Kong (1988).

Chapter 6

'A Burning Problem', from *The Week*, India. July 1983.

Chaudhary, S. N., 'Dowry System: A Historical and Social Review' from *How India*. n.p. (1981).

Kishwar, M. & Vanita, R., (eds) *In Search of Answers: Indian Women's Voices* Zed Press Ltd., London, UK (1984).

Krishnamurthy, S., *The Dowry Problem*. IBJ Prakashana, Bangalore, India (1981).

Manjula, C. G., 'Beasts in Darkness'. *Manushi*. New Delhi, India (1981).

Nayak, Jessie B., *Indian Womanhood, Then and Now – Situation, Efforts, Profiles*. Satprakashan Sanchar Kendra, M.P., India (1983).

Omvedt, Gail, *We Will Smash This Prison! Indian Women in Struggle*. Zed Press, London, UK (1980).

Patel, Vibhuti. 'AWRAN's Alternative Asia Pacific Report on the Impact of the UN Decade for Women'. Country Report for India (1986).

'Prosecution by the Witness'. *Femina*, India (1983).

Sevanti, Ninan & Sanjay Suri, *Why Women Burn – Claustrophobic Homes Strain Conjugal Harmony*. New Delhi, India (1983).

Singh Nalini, 'Why Dowry Spells Death' *Indian Express*, India (1981).

Verghese, Jamila, 'Dowry in Everyday Living'. *The Report on Amendment to the Prohibition of Dowry Act & Protection of Abandoned Women and Children*. New Delhi, India (1979).

'Women and the Law' in *Banhi*, an occasional journal of the Joint Women's Programme, Bangalore, India (1981).

Yadav, Uma, (ed.) *Mahila Dakshata Samiti*. New Delhi, India (n.d).

Chapter 7

Acharya, Meena, *The Status of Women in Nepal*. CEDA, Kathmandu, Nepal (1979).

Anwar, Shamim, *Woman Re-Created*. Lahore, Pakistan (1980).

'Commission on Theology from Third World Women's Perspective'. A Report from Intercontinental Women's Conference, Ecumenical Association of Third World Theologians, Stree, Madras, India (1986).

Eck, Diana L. & Jain, Devaki, *Speaking of Faith, Committee on Women, Religion and Social Change*. New Delhi, India (1986).

Ghimire, Durga, (ed.) *Women and Development*, Centre for Economic Development and Administration, Tribhuvan University, Kathmandu, Nepal, (1977).

Haddad, Yvonne, 'The Image of Women in Contemporary Muslim Literature', Pakistan Women's Institute, Lahore, Pakistan (1983).

Latif, Nargis, 'A Seminar on Chador and Chardiwari'. DAWN, Pakistan (1980).

Majupuria, India, *Nepalese Women*. M. Devi, Kirtipur, Kathmandu, Nepal (1982).

Mernissi, Fatima, *Beyond the Veil*. Al Saqi Books, London, UK (1975).

Park, Sun ai, (ed.) *In God's Image*, Singapore (1987).

'The Quest – Towards an Alternative Perspective on Women in Pakistan'. The Women's Resource and Publication Centre, Lahore, Pakistan (1986).

Rajbhandari, Menaka, 'Some Considerations on Nepalese Women'. Asian Cultural Forum on Development. Bangkok, Thailand (1985).

'A Report on Second Consultation for the Establishment of Feminist Theology in Asia'. Korean Association of Women Theologians (1984).

'The Role of Women in Buddhism'. Thai Inter-Religious Commission for Development (TICD) newsletter, *Seeds of Peace*. Bangkok, Thailand.

Saadawi, Nawal El, *The Hidden Face of Eve – Women in the Arab World*. Zed Press Ltd, London, UK (1988).

Shrestha, Ratna S., 'Legal Status of Nepalese Women'. *Asian Action*, Newsletter of the Asian Cultural Forum on Development (ACFOD), Thailand (1983).

Shrestha, Vijaya, *Women's Decade in Nepal, WSCC National Plan of Action*. Nepal (1984).

'Women's Action Forum'. *Newsletter 6*. Lahore, Pakistan (1985).

Chapter 8

Khaing, Mi Mi, *The World of Burmese Women* Zed Books Ltd, London, UK (1984).

Kha Nau, Lillian, 'Women in Burma'. Paper submitted to Christian Conference of Asia (1982).

Lewin, Kinchida, 'Gender Role in Burmese Society' (1977).

Chapter 9

Asiaweek, March 1986.
Far Eastern Economic Review, March 1986.
'Filipino Women in Struggle'. Task Force Detainees. Manila, Philippines (1984).
'How Do We Liberate Ourselves?' Center for Women's Resources. Manila, Philippines (1987).
Kalaw-Tirol, L., 'The Concerned Women: Tomorrow May Be Too Late'. *Panorama*. Manila, Philippines (1983).
Mercado, Monina A., *People Power*. The James B. Reuter, SJ Foundation. Manila, Philippines (1986).
Newsweek, March 1986.
Tan, Christine, 'The Liberation and Justice Dimension in the Mission of the Local Church'. RGS, Manila, Philippines (1980).
Tavera, Mita P., 'Filipino Women in Crisis'. GABRIELA's Convention Proceedings. Manila, Philippines (1985).
Wynne, Alison, 'No Time For Crying'. Resource Center for Philippine Concerns. Kowloon, Hong Kong (1980).

Chapter 10

Asian Womanhood. Asian Students Association (ANNFSU) newsletter. Nepal (1985).
'Asian Women Speak Out!' The Asian Women's Research & Action Network (AWRAN). Davao City, Philippines (1985).
AWRAN. AWRAN newsletter. Davao, Philippines (1986).
Balai Asian Journal. Manila, Philippines (1981).
Bhasin, Kamla (ed.), *Towards Empowerment*. India (1985).
Bhasin, Kamla & Khan Nighat S., *Feminism and Its Relevance in South Asia*, Kali for Women. New Delhi, India (1986).
Cho, Hyoung, AWRAN, country report. Korea (1985).
Eminist, A. F., 'The Women's Movement in Pakistan'. *The Star*, Pakistan (1983).
'The End Is Just Beginning'. An alternative Philippines report for AWRAN meeting. Davao City, Philippines (1985).
Huang, Nora C. & Chen, Su-Chiu, AWRAN, country report. Taiwan (1985).
Labour Pains. After-5 Collective. Singapore (1984).
Lu, Hsiu-Lien A., 'Women's Liberation Under Martial Law'. USA (1988).
Mayuga, Sylvia L., (ed.) *Babaylan*. CWR, Manila, Philippines (1984).
Ng Cecilia, 'Women in Malaysia – Problems and Issues'. In Park, Sun ai (ed.) *In God's Image*. Singapore (1986).
Santos-Maranan, Aida F., 'Struggling to Break Free'. From *Solidaridad II*, RCPC. Tokyo, Japan (1987).
'Voices of Mindanao Women'. Women's Studies and Resource Center (WSRC). Davao City, Philippines (1988).
Women's Update. GABRIELA National Women's Coalition quarterly newsletter. Manila, Philippines.

Index

Sri Lanka, 1, 5, 6, 28-31, 56, 100; women's
  movement in, 156-7
starvation, 9
sterilization of women, 16
stoning of women, 96
street traders, women as, 68, 113
strikes, 44, 145; in Philippines, 45-7
Suda, 82
sugar plantations, 31
suicide, 67, 68, 75, 77, 79, 80, 82, 83, 86, 90
Suzuki, Zenko, 153
Swain, Betty Sisk, ii

Tabata, Sawako, 158
Tagiwalo, Judy, 112-13
Taiwan, i, 5, 102, 130; women's
  movement in, 152-3
Taiwan Independence and Democracy
  Movement, 152
Takeyama, Michio, 103
Tamil peoples, 21
Tamil women, 29-31
Tan, Sister Christine, 123-9
Tavera, Mita, 119-20
tea, 31
tea plantations, 28-31
teachers, women as, 106
'teahouses', 64-6
textile industry, 37
Thai-Burma railway, 27
Thailand, 3, 5, 27, 56, 62-9, 72, 74, 100,
  109, 153
Thalidomide, 2
Third World Women Against
  Exploitation, 144
Tong-il Textile Company, 149
Tores, Edith, 144
torture, 83, 113, 125, 134, 139, 150, 151
tourism, 65
trade unions, 19, 24, 25, 35, 37, 39, 46, 47,
  56
Tse, Christine, 43-4
tuberculosis, 121, 135
turnover of women workers, 37

unemployment, 17, 60, 117
United Kingdom, 10
United Nations Fund for Population
  Activities, 15
United Nations Women's Decade, 3, 7,
  60, 98, 144, 151, 152, 153, 156
United Nations Women's Decade
  International Conference, 32
United States Aid, 15
United States of America (USA), 31, 145
untouchables, 25, 86
US naval bases, 72

US soldiers, sexual needs of, 72

veil, wearing of, 13, 97, 98, 99, 109
venereal disease, 65, 72, 73, 90
Verghese, Jamila, 81
Vietnam, 1, 3, 5
Vietnam War, 66, 72, 73
violence: against wives, 25; against
  women, 54, 56, 73, 152, 154, 157;
  family, 68
virgin girls, 65
vitamin deficiency, 11
Voices of Women (Sri Lanka), 157

wages, 47, 60; non-payment of, 56; of
  women, 28, 29, 31, 32, 35, 36, 39, 42,
  50, 51, 53, 57, 66, 67, 68, 70, 73
waitresses, 66
water, carrying of, 8, 29, 91, 111
whipping of women, 6, 96, 146, 147
widows, remarriage of, 82
Wichiencharoen, Kanitha, 64, 68
women: abuse of, 50-61; and Islam, 94;
  and Japanese-style management,
  41-4; and religion, 89-102; as artisans,
  107; as cheap labour, 3; as doctors,
  104; as factory workers, 113, 132, 145;
  as journalists, 113; as migrants, 157; as
  property, 78; as street traders, 107,
  113; as teachers, 106; at university, 81;
  Buddhist concept of, 100-1; Chinese,
  33; Confucian concept of, 101;
  contempt for, 87-8; health of, 18;
  Hindu concept of, 92-4; in agricultural
  labour, 108; in prison, 113, 150, 152; in
  sport, 95; Indian, 6, 33; isolation of,
  50-61; Japanese, 4; Japanese concept
  of, 38; Malay, 33; migrant, 50-61;
  obedience required of, 88; role of, 93;
  rural, in Bangladesh, 13-14;
  segregation from men under Islam, 95;
  sexual exploitation of, 62-74; sexual
  power of, 99; trafficking in, 74; United
  States, 4; working conditions of, 46, 60
Women and Development Asia Pacific
  Center (Bangkok), 110
Women for Equality and Peace (South
  Korea), 133, 148, 151-2
women plantation workers, 21-32
women tea pickers, 28
women workers: in factories, 21-32, 44; in
  Japan, 41; low status of, 42; part-time,
  42
Women's Action Forum (Pakistan)
  (WAF), 96, 146-8
Women's Aid Organization (WAO)
  (Malaysia), 153-4